Life Flies
When You're
Having Fun

AMONG OTHER BOOKS BY
JERRY B. JENKINS

NONFICTION
General

As You Leave Home: Parting Thoughts from a Loving Parent
Twelve Things I Want My Kids to Remember Forever
Hedges: Loving Your Marriage Enough to Protect It
Rekindled: How to Keep the Warmth in Marriage

Biographies

Sammy Tippit	Meadowlark Lemon
Hank Aaron	George Sweeting
Dick Motta	Christine Wyrtzen
Pat Williams	Deanna McClary
Paul Anderson	Orel Hershiser
Madeline Manning	Joe Gibbs
B.J. Thomas	Mike Singletary
Walter Payton	Nolan Ryan
Luis Palau	Bill Gaither

FICTION
Adult

The Margo Mysteries
The Jennifer Grey Mysteries
The Operative
Rookie
The Deacon's Woman

Children

The Bradford Family Adventures
Dallas O'Neil and the Baker Street Sports Club
The Dallas O'Neil Mysteries
The Tara Chadwick Books

Life Flies When You're Having Fun

Jerry B. Jenkins

VICTOR BOOKS

A DIVISION OF SCRIPTURE PRESS PUBLICATIONS INC.
USA CANADA ENGLAND

Unless otherwise indicated, all Scripture references are from the
Holy Bible, New International Version®. Copyright © 1973, 1978, 1984
by International Bible Society. Used by permission of Zondervan
Publishing House. All rights reserved. Other quotations are from the
Authorized (King James) Version.

Copyediting: Barbara Williams
Cover Design: Scott Rattray
Cover Illustration: Robert Bergin

Library of Congress Cataloging-in-Publication Data
Jenkins, Jerry B.
   Life flies when you're having fun / by Jerry B. Jenkins.
       p.   cm.
    ISBN 1-56476-126-6
    1. Jenkins, Jerry B. 2. Christian biography — United States.
I. Title.
BR1725.J388A3   1993
209'.2 — dc20
[B]   92-41363
                                                 CIP

**Published in association with the literary agency of Alive Communi-
cations, P.O. Box 49068, Colorado Springs, Colorado 80949.**

1 2 3 4 5 6 7 8 9 10 Printing / Year 97 96 95 94 93

DEDICATION

In loving memory of Fred Quade

CONTENTS

NO NEW MESSAGES?

I have been collecting snatches of things I've heard — from my youngest, Michael, asking if "Shut up" is one of the Ten Commandments (you'll be pleased to know I told him the truth) — to the Voice Mailbox greeting I get frequently.

Voice Mailbox is the name of our office's electronic system for sending and receiving messages, an answering machine with a fascinating array of features. I love the system, but here's my problem. After I have listened to my messages, a pleasant female voice comes on and informs me, "You have no more new messages."

The first few times it happened, I thought, *How interesting. How handy. I appreciate knowing that I have come to the end of my messages.*

Yet something niggled at my brain and depressed me. I wondered if it was that I was lonely or felt rejected because I had no more new messages.

Then it hit me. What bothered me was that my brain translated the word messages as "things to say," rather than "things to hear."

Therefore, several times a day, I'm bombarded with an unintentionally negative bit of news. It mocks me, taunts me, threatens me. Is it possible? I have no more new messages. I have nothing more to say.

Pity the poor pastor who installs one of these machines. At least twice on Sunday and once in the middle of the week, he must have a new message.

I wonder if these machines can be reprogrammed to have the pleasant voice say, "You have no more new telephone messages, but, boy, do you have a lot to say! Get to work and say it!"

I don't sing or dance or preach. But at the risk of writing a lot without saying much, I leave what I have to say to your judgment. Thanks for taking the time.

Jerry B. Jenkins

A BETTER STORY
...AND TRUE

DON'T LET YOUR CHILDREN SEE THIS—not if you are letting them enjoy the Santa Claus myth.

I was one who bought the Santa story hook, line, and sack full of goodies. That wasn't my parents' fault. They couldn't know how serious it was to me. My older brothers grew out of believing in Santa, no one realizing that I still carried the torch for the story.

And what a story! Be good and you get stuff from a guy who seemed somewhat like God. Blasphemous? Not if the story was true. This guy could deliver toys to the house of every good kid in the world in twenty-four hours!

I not only believed Santa would visit my house, but I was also convinced that he would not come until I was sound asleep. And there was no fooling Santa. Once I lay perfectly still with my eyes shut for several minutes, only to peek when I thought I heard footsteps on the roof. Of course, Santa immediately left, busy in some other neighborhood until the Jenkins kid was really out.

In kindergarten, other Santa believers looked up to me because when consulted, I took their side. The fact that more and more peers wavered in their faith might have rattled me, had it not been for a chat I had with the jolly elf himself.

I sat on his lap in a department store, awed and scared, knowing he was the true Santa. All the others I had seen on street corners and in other stores were his helpers. He asked what I wanted, and I told him. He asked if I had been good, and I nodded.

Then he said his elves had told him that I didn't always finish my green beans. I nearly died. It was true — I *was* guilty. (But I have loved green beans ever since. Honest.)

How could I know that my dad had whispered this news to "Santa" when I was distracted? And how could Dad have known that this conversation locked into my soul the belief that it was all true?

The day finally came, much later in my life than it should have (around age seven), when the evidence was too great to ignore. When I put the question to my dad, he said, "You don't honestly still believe in Santa Claus, do you?"

"Yes," I said, and argued the point for a while, profoundly disappointed. I was too young at the time to articulate my greater fear—that I would soon hear that the Jesus story wasn't true either.

Eventually, of course, I learned. Santa was like Mother Goose or the Easter Bunny. I never believed in them.

Jesus is unique. He is God, Son of God, the Savior of mankind, and one day became my Savior.

In my early teens, my pastor chatted with the youth group and told us it was time we understood more about the mystery. He explained what it meant that Mary had been a virgin. He explained that though Jesus was just one Man, His divinity allowed His death to pay the sin penalty for all who would believe and receive.

The best part of the Jesus story, the Gospel, was

that it was available to all—the naughty as well as the nice. Even if the Santa story had been true, it didn't compare to God's idea.

Angels, a miraculous birth, a star, dreams, warnings, sinlessness. Death, burial, resurrection, life eternal. Ah, that would be a great story even if it were made up. Even better than Santa.

How much better that it's true.

With our own children, Dianna and I weren't killjoys. Our kids were free to enjoy all the magic and fun and excitement of Christmas, including the legends and myths. But we made it clear from day one that Santa was make-believe. Santa was like the Easter Bunny or Mother Goose.

And while we coached them not to spoil the fun of believing in Santa for other kids (which in truth protected us from their parents), we took every opportunity to remind them: Jesus is real. His is the best story of all.

A FEW MORE DAYS

AT TIMES I WISH I LOOKED FORWARD to the return of Christ with as much excitement as I looked forward to a delivery when I was seven years old.

What is it about that most wondrous of all promises that makes some hope it doesn't happen until after next week's ball game or until they are married, have children, get promoted, accomplish something?

Scripture is clear that to be with Christ "is far better," but that remains a mystery. Even with all the scholars in Christendom, we know little about heaven. We know what will be there (light and splendor) and what will not (darkness), and we know we will have glorified minds and bodies (I can get excited about that). I'm confident we won't be bored, but try explaining that to a six-year-old who doesn't want to go to heaven because "I like my bed."

I admire those who genuinely look forward to the return of Christ or their own home goings because they long to be with their Savior. They look forward with eager anticipation, waiting, watching for that great day.

I have waited for good things in my life, sometimes for things that never came. Some came and didn't satisfy. But never have I waited and anticipated and hoped and prayed for anything the way I did when I was seven.

My dad was a city police officer with a wife and three boys, and although we were not poverty-stricken, we enjoyed few extras. Someday I'll have to ask Dad how he managed it. He either saved (likely), borrowed (unlikely), or got a bonus (implausible). Anyway, he piled us into the car, and we went to a shop where we looked at used bicycles. We didn't hope for the gorgeous new ones; we didn't even beg. It isn't that we were that wonderful; we were simply realistic.

Somewhere in the sales pitch the bike man allowed that if Dad could see his way to purchase three brand-new Schwinns, it would cost him very little more than three good used bikes. Eyes wide, mouths agape, we heard Dad tell the man he had a deal.

Big brother Jim was fitted for a full-sized red one. Jeff got an identical one, but green. Mine was identical to Jeff's but small. Beauties, they would be sent to our home the next day.

When the blue pickup arrived, the two big bikes were delivered. It would be a "few more days" for mine. Did anyone understand what that meant to a seven-year-old?

For days I raced home after school to see if my bike had arrived. More than once I chased a blue pickup down our street only to see it pass our house. One Saturday I sprinted till I was out of breath and saw the truck pull into our driveway and leave—with my bike aboard—because no adult was home to take the delivery.

That was the worst. I didn't know bike trucks didn't make Sunday deliveries. But when I got home from school Monday, Mom sent me to the garage. There it was, lined up with Jim's and Jeff's. But still I couldn't ride it. I had forgotten that bikes were delivered without air in the tires.

I walked the bike around, not allowed to sit on it till Dad got home and could run it up to the filling station for air. Then I rode so much during the half-hour before dark that I was delightfully sore for days. All that waiting and hoping, the disappointments, and the final delay had made my treasure only more cherished.

More than thirty-five years later I remember the deep ache of longing for that promise and the joy of its coming. That's the way I want to feel about the coming of Christ.

AND TO ALL
A GOOD NIGHT

AFTER CHRISTMAS MANY YEARS AGO, three elementary-school-aged boys played with their new toys until they were tired of them — three days or so.

Their mother brought an empty cardboard box into the dining room, sat the boys down, and told them of underprivileged boys at a local orphanage who each got a piece of fruit, a candy bar, a comb, and a cheap toy in a standard package.

"Merry Christmas," one of the brothers said with sarcasm.

Their mother nodded, brows arched. "How about we give some of those guys a Christmas they won't forget?"

They sat silent. She continued.

"Let's fill this box with toys that will make Christmas special. We'll do what Jesus would do."

One of the brothers had an idea. "With all my new stuff, I don't need all my old stuff!"

He ran to get armloads full of dingy, dilapidated toys, but when he returned, his mother's look stopped him. "Is that what Jesus would do?"

He pursed his lips and shrugged. "You want us to give our new stuff?"

"It's just a suggestion."

"All of it?"

"I didn't have in mind all of it. Just whatever toys you think."

"I'll give this car," one said, placing it in the box.

"If you don't want it," another said. "I'll take it."

"I'm not givin' it to you; I'm givin' it to the orphans."

"I'm done with this bow and arrow set," another said.

"I'll take that," another chimed in.

"I'll trade you these pens for that model."

"No deal, but I'll take the pens and the cap gun."

The boys hardly noticed their mother leave the room. The box sat there, empty and glaring. The boys idly slipped away and played on the floor. But there was none of the usual laughing, arguing, roughhousing. Each played with his favorite toys with renewed vigor.

One by one the boys visited the kitchen. It was a small house and that was the only place their mother could be.

Each found her sitting at the table, her coat and hat and gloves on. Her face had that fighting tears look. No words were exchanged.

The boys got the picture. She wasn't going to browbeat her sons into filling that box. No guilt trips, no pressure. It had been just a suggestion. Each returned to play quietly, as if in farewell to certain toys. And to selfishness.

A few minutes later, their mother came for the box. The eldest had carefully and resolutely placed almost all his new toys in it. The others selected more carefully but chose the best for the box.

Their mother took the box to the car without a word, an expression, or a gesture. She never reported on the reception of the orphans, and she was never asked.

Several years of childhood remained, but childishness had been dealt a blow.

WITH WINGS
AS CHICKENS

I WAS ONE OF THOSE KIDS who didn't want to go to summer camp. Maybe it had to do with my place in the family—third of three boys at that time. Maybe it had to do with a general childhood fear of abandonment.

I had no reason to fear that. My parents were close to each other and to us kids. But that didn't keep me from fear of the dark or fear of losing them if we got separated in a huge store. Somewhere deep down inside each child is a dread terror that he may never see his parents again.

A child may be cantankerous and even rebellious around Mom or Dad, but when he is not with them, he feels out of sorts. He is relieved only when he is reunited with them.

I don't know when we outgrow that. My own eight-year-old recently cried, "I would never want to be sent to an orphanage like in Anne of Green Gables!"

Once when I was almost thirteen, I panicked when my dad didn't show up at a prearranged time and place. I was old enough to make a call or approach an authority, of course, but my first reaction was visceral, fundamental.

I recall my first day of kindergarten. I had longed to go to school with my brothers for as long as I could remember. I loved to look at their schoolbooks and pretend to do homework with them. But I also had a daily routine that gave me lots of time alone with my mother. I didn't realize how much that meant to me until I started going to school in the mornings.

She had told me long in advance that she would walk me to school and to my room. She said she would make sure I was all set before she left. She promised to be there when school was out. "I know you're a big boy," she said, "and you'll do just fine."

So I resolved not to cry. I had an image to maintain. I was almost five, and she had convinced me I would do well.

When that day came, my mother could probably tell I had less bounce in my step, less eagerness to get to school than I had shown before. But I swallowed that lump in my throat. I wanted to smile and was frustrated that I couldn't, but I would not give in to tears, despite the many sobbing children in that room.

The mothers all stood at the door, smiling and waving. I can still remember what my mother wore that day, and I can still see her looking right into my eyes. I knew she supported me and I knew she would be there at the end of the morning, but still it was painful. Of course, by the next day, I wanted to walk to school with my brothers.

Camp, though, was something else again. A week away from home, no contact with parents except by mail. My brothers would be there, but I wouldn't share a bunk with either of them. I would be on a team with kids my own age. This would be very educational.

I can't say for certain that my rheumatic fever at age eight wasn't partly psychosomatic. It put off my first week at camp until I was nine.

Again I didn't cry. But I hated growing up. Within a few days I had learned to interact with strangers, fascinated that other kids went to similar churches and had a like faith. I still missed my parents and my home, and if I'd had to choose, I probably would not have gone.

But the next year, I was ready to go again. By the time I was a teenager, I was working at camp for the summer. Some of my richest personal experiences with God happened there, and I made decisions that shaped my future.

Sometimes it takes being away from home to push us to faith and dependence on a new source of security. Like mother eagles pushing their own offspring from the nest, our parents nudge us into the unknown. On the wings of their prayers, we frantically flap and flutter toward the One who will never abandon us.

For He Himself has said, "Never will I leave you; never will I forsake you" (Heb. 13:5).

WITHOUT A CLUE

HAVE YOU EVER THOUGHT that a person was so obnoxious, so unpleasant, so caustic, or such a big mouth that he or she had to be acting that way on purpose? Some people are so offensive they seem to have it honed to a science.

It shouldn't come as a shock to me—though it always does—that most such people are completely unaware of how they come across. When you find yourself wondering, *Why doesn't that guy care what others think?* consider that he probably does. He is simply unaware.

I'll never forget how stunned I was as a youngster to learn that I was a bigmouth. I didn't have a clue. I didn't notice that I jabbered all the time, dominated conversations, and likely was the target of many rolled eyes from adults.

In third or fourth grade, I was in a Sunday School class with one of my brothers, who was as quiet as I was talkative. I recall enjoying the class, and myself, immensely. I assumed everyone else was having a good time too.

Then one day my Sunday School teacher happened to visit our home. He was an old friend of my parents, simply making a social call. But in the course of the conversation I got a glimpse of myself.

My teacher was commenting, in passing, about the differences in kids' personalities, even within the same family. "Like this one," he said, pointing to my brother. "You hardly ever hear a peep from him."

I was about to pipe up that my brother was just shy, when I remembered that he thought that was an insult and would probably resent it. Then my teacher nodded toward me and added, "And this one never shuts up."

It was not said maliciously, and not intended as a message for me. The adults all chuckled and shook their heads at his interesting point, but I was stunned speechless. For once.

It was as if the whole quarter in that Sunday School class flashed before my eyes. I saw myself wanting to answer every question, read every passage, comment on every story. The biggest revelation was that the teacher had a different view of me than I thought he had. I wasn't a precocious, interested Bible student. I was one of those crazy, bigmouthed kids.

That changed my behavior in Sunday School for a while, but I was a slow learner. In high school I noticed the vacant look in the eyes of one of the "cool" guys as I talked to him, so I asked, "Have I told you this story before?"

"Only about twenty times," he said and walked away.

Another time, sitting with a bunch of guys after basketball practice, I held forth long enough to prompt my brother (yes, the quiet one) to say, "Why don't you just be quiet awhile?"

People who are more than talkative, those who are also belligerent or condescending or sarcastic or bullying, are also usually unaware of it. I learned this during my tenure in management. Occasionally, I had to deal with people who were causing discord by their treatment of employees.

Almost invariably, the very personality trait that was alienating their employees was something they considered a strength. A stern taskmaster who was seen as cold and aloof rated himself high on interpersonal skills. One whose staff was about to mutiny told me, "People like to work for me."

When someone points out that we are not coming across well, our first reaction is usually denial. I recall wondering how people could be so wrong about me. But words have a way of rattling around in our brains and working on us. We eventually (I hope) get the message, and then pivotal changes can take place.

We should be thankful for those people who care enough to risk the fallout of loving confrontation. "A word aptly spoken is like apples of gold in settings of silver. Like an earring of gold or an ornament of fine gold is a wise man's rebuke to a listening ear" (Prov. 25:11-12).

TO TELL THE TRUTH

ONE OF THE WORST EXPERIENCES of my childhood was one of the best things that ever happened to me.

My older brother Jeff has always been good with his hands. Not only can he sketch, but he can also fashion things from raw material, just for the fun of it. One day when I was about eight and he nine, he made a toy out of an acorn and a toothpick. It was a common item, but I couldn't have done it, and I envied him.

He left the gadget outside and soon caught me playing with it. There was the typical argument. "That's mine," he said.

"Says who?"

"I made it."

"Did not."

"Did too."

When Mom got involved, I quickly abandoned my "I found it" argument, because that would only prove the toy was Jeff's. I took a more creative tack. "I made it," I said.

No one believed me, of course, but I stuck by my story. Jeff's toy must still be lost, because I had one I had made myself. Jeff gave me a typical brotherly look that told me not only would he never believe me, but also that he knew the truth.

Mom tried every method she knew to get me to confess. She made me look her in the eye and assure her I was telling the truth. She reminded me that lying was a sin. She told me that only God and I knew the truth.

Somehow I mustered the wherewithal to look Mom in the eye and lie to her face. "If I find out you're lying," she said, "I will have to spank you."

"I'm not lying," I lied, "but if I was, how would you find out?"

"You would have to tell me," she said, "how else would I know?"

How true, I thought. And how interesting. Only

I could implicate myself. Yet somehow the knowledge that I held my destiny in my hands did not reassure me.

I didn't last five minutes. The toy quickly lost its appeal. The very sight of it filled me with guilt and remorse. I thought of putting it back where I found it so Jeff could discover it and think he had been wrong. That idea only convinced me I was totally depraved.

I took the toy to my mother's room, where she sat as if expecting me.

"Mommy, I feel terrible!" I blurted. "I lied to you, and you can spank me!"

How I wanted that justice! How I longed to rid myself of that guilt and, most of all, to mend the rift between us.

"Take that back to Jeff while I get a switch," she said.

I ran to him, eager to get the ordeal over with and wondering at Mom's decision to spank me with something other than her hand for the first time. When I returned, she pulled me close and embraced me with one hand, whipping me with that switch in the other.

In truth I hardly felt the whacks through my jeans. We boys were never severely punished. But I wailed at my remorse and over the relationship that had been broken and now was restored. She also urged me to confess my sin to God.

Some will say they are glad that kind of parenting is passé, that it bordered on abuse. I say it changed my life. For all my sins and shortcomings, and I have many, my conscience is pricked even at exaggeration, let alone lying.

That's why it jars me to see advice columnist Abigail Van Buren reassure a mother who lied to protect her son from the police: "Don't be so hard on yourself; you did what most mothers would have done. . . ."

And that's why I hate the telephone company commercial in which the wife uses the caller ID gadget to give her husband time to duck out the front door so she can tell his boss, "You just missed him."

"You shall not bear false witness" is unequivocal from the Book of books. I'll be eternally grateful that my mother didn't let me get away with a lie. We could use more parenting like that.

OF BULLIES
AND BROTHERS

SECOND SAMUEL 22:3 SAYS I CAN TRUST in "God my rock . . . my shield and the horn of my salvation. . . . My stronghold, my refuge . . . my Savior," who saves me from violence. What a comforting thought in this age!

When I was in fifth grade, God once provided my refuge in the form of my big brother, though Jim probably doesn't even remember it.

I was being terrorized by a bully. "Richard" had been held back three times (in those days we said he had flunked). So he should have been in eighth grade, and he looked the part. He came to school in a black leather jacket.

While none of us had actually seen him hurt anyone, legends abounded. We heard he'd been in gang fights and rumbles. Once several dozen of us gathered to watch a fight, only to see a teacher break it up before it began.

What stayed with me from that was the fear on Richard's opponent's face, then the relief when he was rescued. Richard betrayed no fear.

I steered clear of Richard until the day he strayed into the path of my snowball. Fortunately for me the school day was beginning and I sprinted into the building, hollering an apology over my shoulder.

Richard caught me in the hall and told me where to meet him after school. "I have to beat you up for that," he said.

I nodded numbly. The rest of that day I lived in fear, as if a contract had been taken out on my life. I had no plan and prayed without hope. I dreaded the end of school like a death penalty. Was it possible he would forget? Could I slip home quickly?

Not a chance. He met me at the first cross street and calmly asked me where I wanted it. Where I wanted it? I tried to apologize again, to explain. He insisted, "Where, Jenkins?"

"Across the street?" I suggested. He nodded and followed me.

No way would I just stand there and take it. A faint glimmer of hope came to me as we crossed. I would take off running and head straight home. He was bigger, stronger, faster, so I would have to surprise him and somehow outrun him for four blocks, the last one downhill.

I caught a break when a couple of little girls somehow got between us as we reached the other side. I dashed madly away, slipping and sliding on the snow-packed sidewalk, running past the warnings of the crossing guard at the next corner, Richard close behind.

Frantic and panting, I charged on, suddenly realizing that I could never make it all the way home at that speed. Richard seemed nearly an adult. He would catch me for sure. Finally I had to slow to a walk to catch my breath. I whirled around to see where he was, and he was gone.

A block-and-a-half from home I spotted him hiding behind a tree up ahead, waiting for me. I had no choice; I would have to surprise him again. I walked slowly, my chest heaving, till I got near the tree, then I took off again. I had surprised him again, but he was soon only a step behind.

My house was in sight, but I couldn't get there.

That's when my big brother appeared from the house. Jim was in junior high, the same age as Richard, but even bigger, stronger, tougher.

"He's after me, Jim!" I gasped. "Get 'im!"

Jim squinted in surprise that anyone but he could have a problem with me. Richard skidded to a stop in our driveway as I escaped inside. I peeked out, almost feeling sorry for Richard. He looked up at Jim and suddenly didn't seem so huge and menacing.

"You picked on the wrong guy," Jim told him, clutching Richard's jacket and pulling him close. He would have none of Richard's halting assurances that he was only kidding, only playing around, that he wouldn't really have done anything to me.

That, Jim said, was good. "Because I'll be checking with him every day. You hurt him, I hurt you."

I never had any more trouble with Richard. In my brother Jim I had a shield and defender equal to any crisis. Thank God.

WEATHER OR NOT

IT WAS A FIFTH-GRADER'S DREAM. Our school had been struck by lightning.

We didn't allow ourselves to believe it until we raced through the tiny community of Oakwood in Kalamazoo, Michigan, that spring of 1960 to see for ourselves. What we saw along the way convinced us it was true.

It wasn't just other kids running back home, their eyes huge, their countenances joyous. Rather, it was century-old trees—six, seven, and eight feet in diameter—that had been uprooted in several yards, crashing through roofs and flattening the occasional car or truck.

After all the times our parents had spirited us to the cellar in the face of tornado warnings, we had stayed in our rooms that night when the worst storm came. No one really knew what happened until morning.

I'll always believe I was awakened by the thunder from the very stroke of lightning that did the deed on Oakwood Elementary. The crack was so loud and so fast that the light still seemed strong in the middle of the night when my eyes popped open.

I love thunderstorms. My favorite time is when the tempest settles overhead and the lightning and thunder assault the senses nonstop. I've been startled awake by nearby clappers, which is no fun, but once I have my senses about me, I can appreciate the power, the noise, the spectacle.

But the explosion from that middle-of-the-night bolt of lightning was so numbing it is hard to describe. Our school was four blocks away, yet the sound alone on our block broke several windows. It was as if something huge and unspeakable had fallen on the pavement right in front of our house.

All it was, was sound. It slammed angrily off anything in its path, echoing and rumbling until we heard its echo miles away. It wasn't until morning, however, that we knew the storm had been any-thing different. We lived in the Midwest. Wonder-ful, thunderfull storms were part of life.

Because it all happened in the middle of the night, no tornadoes were spotted. But in the morning no one could deny that we had been visit-ed by something, once we saw all those monstrous trees in incongruous repose, block after block.

No one died, and few were injured. Back then, most people after midnight were either asleep or working the graveyard shift. There was property damage, of course, but none so great as at my school. Yet nature provided little respite for antsy ten- and eleven-year-olds. We were soon marched up the street to the unscathed junior high where we were provided a room for several weeks.

I thought of that storm when funnels ripped through northern Illinois recently, killing two doz-en and injuring nearly 300. Disasters seem remote and other-worldly until you see on the news a de-molished church or school you've driven past, and you realize that the people grieving and picking up the pieces are almost close enough to be your neighbors.

Being a husband and father made me look upon this storm with much different eyes than those that were wide with wonder in 1960, hoping the storm had brought a reprieve from school. I found myself empathizing with parents who searched frantically for their children, who picked through rubble and wondered how they would ever reconstruct their homes.

Somehow the proximity of the disaster made it more real to me than even my childhood memories, and I appreciated my home and my family in an altogether fresh way. I don't understand tragedy or natural calamity any more than anyone else, but I do know that those of us who are spared must once again consider the fragility of our existences and ponder how we will redeem the time.

"You do not even know what will happen tomorrow. What is your life? You are a mist that appears for a little time and then vanishes" (James 4:14).

GRATEFUL FOR GRACE

WHEN I WAS IN ELEMENTARY SCHOOL, my dad once took my brothers and me to the home of a crotchety old man who said that one of us had thrown a rock through his window.

I had not done it, but all the way to the man's house, fear gripped me. What if he said he had seen me? Would my father believe me? I knew I would look and sound guilty.

"If you didn't do it, you have nothing to fear," Dad said. "No one can be hurt by the truth."

True enough, but any one of us could have been hurt by an old man who mistook us for someone else.

"Tell me which one did it," my dad told the man, "and we'll make it right."

The man studied our faces and admitted he had been mistaken. The ride home was much more pleasant.

A few years later, when I was a high school freshman, I was unjustly accused. But now I was at school, dealing with an angry, beefy football coach, and my dad was not there as a mediator. Although I was innocent, I felt scared and guilty.

I had broken my arm during one of the first few weeks of freshman football practice. I watched the rest of the season in a cast, but grew bored hanging around. So I helped the equipment managers. It wasn't my assignment. I could come and go as I pleased. It was just something to do.

When someone left a mess of wet towels in the locker room one day, the coach exploded. To avoid that ex-military man and his legendary 5-foot paddle — which he swung with both hands and which had launched more than one malcontent headfirst into the lockers — the real equipment managers somehow succeeded in laying the blame at my feet. Which I learned as I innocently walked in on the scene. Picture a beet-red coach and several pale, quaking managers.

"Grab your ankles, Jenkins," the coach bellowed. "I'll teach you to leave a mess like this."

I protested that I wasn't even a manager, that I was an injured player, but that I would be happy to clean it up anyway. I searched the eyes of my accusers and knew they were only protecting their own hides.

The coach didn't stall. "Grab 'em!"

Only my left arm reached the ankle. My right hung suspended, bent rigid in the plaster. Upside down, I could see between my knees the coach sweeping back that gigantic paddle. I heard the whoosh and saw the wide eyes of the guilty. I shut my eyes and tried not to tighten.

The paddle stopped inches from my seat, and the coach tapped me ever so lightly with it. He smiled. "You're not a manager," he said. "You are an injured player!"

I nearly collapsed with relief. When the coach ordered the managers to line up for their punishment, I quickly cleaned up the wet towels. There's something about a reprieve that makes one benevolent, even when the punishment would have been unjust.

I have been unjustly accused a few other times. I hurt the worst when my motives are questioned, or when I am accused of lying. If I support an unpopular decision, I may be charged with a personal vendetta. That can cause deep pain.

All such experiences force me to think of the grossest case of unjust accusation in history, when a Man who knew no sin became sin for us, that we might become the righteousness of God in Him (2 Cor. 5:21). Not only had He done no wrong, but He was righteousness personified. And not only was He wrongly accused, He was also put to death.

Thinking about the ultimate sacrifice by the epitome of innocence puts our puny trials into perspective. And realizing that Jesus died on our behalf in spite of our unworthiness should also affect our self-images. Rather than impressing us with ourselves, it should leave us grateful for grace.

JUST DO IT

I RECENTLY FOLLOWED THE ADVICE of the NIKE athletic equipment company and simply did it.

For years I had been thinking about trying to get together with the ragtag bunch of eleven- and twelve-year-olds with whom I played Little League baseball in the early 1960s. When I was back in Kalamazoo, Michigan, in the fall of 1990 for the 75th anniversary of my childhood church, the nostalgia bug hit me hard.

Two things make my Little League recollection unique: we won the state championship in 1962, and my family moved to another state the next year.

My rich, deep, crystal-clear memories of those

wonderful, tension-filled, single-elimination tour-
naments have never dulled, even though I didn't
stay to grow up with those kids. I haven't seen
them since the early summer of 1963, but we were
childhood friends and enjoyed an astounding experience together.

I remember the scores and highlights of all fourteen tournament games.

I can tell you who pitched and who made the
key hits and scored the winning runs.

Not surprisingly, no one cares but the players.
Although they are now men, they are etched onto
my brain as children. Our voices had not even
changed when I moved away.

I got an address and wrote one of the former
team members. He wrote back. Of course he remembered. And here are some more addresses.
From those I got others, and phone numbers.

I sent a tentative letter to several: I'm going to
be in town for a wedding in March, I said. Any
interest in a reunion? I asked the local paper to
help me locate everyone.

I've been stunned by the response. Letters,
faxes, phone calls—everyone is excited, even the

coach, retired in Florida. "I'll come anywhere, anytime to see my boys!" he says.

Strangest have been the phone calls. These guys are not just older and more mature. They're middle-aged.

My mind's eye pictures skinny little bodies, teeth too big for tiny faces, high, squeaky voices — "Jenks, we're playin' behind the school. Can you come?" We're older now than our fathers were the last time we saw one another. The voices on the phone, incongruously, are those of men — not Little Leaguers. Yes, it's the voices that rock me most. I don't know what I expected: adults with the voices of children?

When I drove to the old neighborhood recently to scout out spots for the reunion, I saw a friend who has been married twenty years to my first girlfriend. Their daughter is a freshman in college, five years older than I was when I moved away. How wonderful to see them, and how strange to have missed their adolescence, early adulthood, even their thirties.

My friends are twelve in my mind, and now I see them not only fully grown, but also with faces and hair color that (like mine) give evidence of the years.

I am eager for the reunion scheduled for next month. A couple of these guys went to elementary school with Bill Hybels, now pastor of America's second largest church. Another—probably my closest friend as a child—is an active Christian, a lay singer whose brother has been preaching for twenty-five years. I first learned that he too was a Christian when we were in second grade, and he blurted, "Are you saved?"

Do you have some long-lost friends or acquaintances who would warm your heart if your could see them again? Have you been thinking about looking them up, wondering if they would remember or be at all interested?

Just do it.

VANCE HAVNER LATE

VANCE HAVNER became a country preacher as a child and proclaimed the message of Christ for decades before his death a few years ago.

I had heard the old man preach and loved his little witticisms. At the great Torrey-Gray Auditorium at Moody in Chicago he held forth at Founder's Week in the dead of winter one February. He was a bit late, and when introduced came hurrying up the aisle to the platform.

"I'd rather be Vance Havner late," he said, "than the late Vance Havner."

The place was packed and the boilers were working overtime, so one of the windows had been opened to equalize the heat. That sent a chill to the platform.

Brother Havner stopped and asked if the window could be shut. "I'm afraid I'm too old for the draft."

He was also the one who said, "The problem with the typical morning worship service is that it starts at 11 o'clock sharp and ends at 12 o'clock dull."

He was elderly by the time I met him, a thin, frail man, poor of hearing and of sight.

He and I had talked only by phone before that meeting, and he was not expecting a young man more than 100 pounds heavier than I am today. After we shook hands he looked me up and down and said, not unkindly, "You're a big kid, ain'tcha?"

"Yes, sir," I said.

"Have you heard about the new garlic sandwich diet?"

"*Garlic* sandwiches?"

"Yeah. You don't lose any weight, but you look a little smaller from a distance."

Humor was merely a tool for Vance Havner. He lived to preach. Virtually self-taught and trained, he became widely sought and traveled the country. His style was homey and anecdotal, but he was so rooted in Scripture that he might have been mistaken for a devoted expositor.

One of his great themes was the insidious sin that sneaks up on the man who thinks himself wise. "The very thing he thinks is a strength is his worst weakness," Havner would say.

I was reminded of that when I recalled an incident from my childhood thirty years ago. I shared a bedroom with my little brother and so was not allowed to keep the light on after his bedtime.

One night after he fell asleep I hit upon a scheme that would allow me to read without bothering him. My big brother had fashioned in shop class a lamp that glowed with blue bulbs. I set that close to my book and read for a couple of hours in the eerie low light.

After I had turned out the lamp and slept for a couple of hours, I awoke in pain. My eyes were red and nearly swollen shut. I awoke my parents, afraid I was going blind. Had I strained my eyes, reading in the low, blue light?

Worse than that, I had been unaware that my brother's creation was an ozone lamp. It emitted ozone gas, which was virtually harmless unless one was careless enough to hover over it for two hours.

The very thing I thought was allowing me to see in the dark could have blinded me, had I not grown weary of reading. I recovered and there was no residual damage, but the doctor told me I had come dangerously close to serious injury.

That seemingly unrelated memory made me think of Vance Havner because it proved one of his favorite points: Beware that thing that makes you think you're wise. It may make you the biggest fool of all.

"Although they knew God, they neither glorified Him as God, nor gave thanks to Him, but their thinking became futile and their foolish hearts were darkened. Although they claimed to be wise, they became fools and exchanged the glory of the immortal God for images made to look like mortal man. . . . They exchanged the truth of God for a lie, and worshiped and served created things rather than the Creator—who is forever praised" (Rom. 1:21-25).

YE OLDE MODERNE
TRANSLATIONETH

AT THE OAKWOOD BIBLE CHURCH in Kalamazoo, Michigan, we were nondenominational and independent, but I wasn't aware of that until after we'd moved away when I was a teenager.

That's the way it should be, I think. Ours was an evangelical, fundamental church, and we probably even leaned toward the blindly patriotic. But we kids weren't aware of it. Our pastor preached Christ and Him crucified, and we got the basics down cold.

In the early '60s when Kenneth Taylor came out with the *Living Letters* — percursor to the *Living Gospels, Living New Testament,* and eventually *The Living Bible* — I recall the news hitting our church like a refreshing breath of air. There was no controversy, no hand-wringing, no thought that his helpful little tool was meant to replace the real Bible.

It seemed everyone had a copy or two of the green and white *Living Letters,* and though it appeared to have been written for children, I recall adults carrying them around too and actually reading them.

All of our memorizing had been done from the *King James.* And while the cadence and poetic style somehow made it easier, I confess there were many verses that were stamped on my mind but not in my heart until many years later when I learned what they meant.

I spent almost three weeks in the hospital when I was eight and my mother took advantage of the time to help me memorize the third chapter of the Gospel of John.

For the most part, I understood and enjoyed the story of the religious leader Nicodemus, visiting Jesus by night. But it didn't surprise me that Nicodemus had trouble understanding what Jesus was saying.

Nicodemus was instructed by Jesus to "marvel

not." Let me tell you, I marveled.

The whole chapter, of course, is filled with the mysteries of God. I was content to accept and believe that one day I would understand all the talk of being born of water and of the Spirit. That wasn't as much of a problem as simply the wording and style of verse 8:

The wind bloweth where it listeth, and thou hearest the sound thereof, but canst not tell whence it cometh, and whither it goeth: so is every one that is born of the Spirit (KJV).

Had I been asked what that meant, I would have answered the way my nine-year-old did when I asked him the same question after he recited his umpteenth AWANA memory verse:

"Don't ask me!"

The key, of course, if we are going to insist that children still memorize from centuries-old translations, is to teach them what the words mean.

My dad made John 3:8 clear to me when he said, "You can hear the wind, but you can't see it." Oh.

Some new versions are closer to being word-for-word translations (a literal word-for-word translation would not be readable in English); others are considered more thought-for-thought.

All translations have their strengths and weaknesses, and people have their favorites and their pariahs. Still, we can rejoice that God has protected His inspired Word through the generations.

As you encourage your children to memorize it and meditate on it, use the translation that will stick in their minds, and explain every word.

MOM'S OLD BIBLE

LATE ONE NIGHT when I was a teenager, I took a good look at my mother's old Bible. The crumbling cover and dog-eared pages brought back memories of bedtime prayers. I thought of Mom when she was Mommy.

An inscription from Dad dates the Bible from before my birth. Mom's maiden name was barely readable on the cover.

Two references were penned onto the dirty first page. One — John 3:5 — is unmistakably written by my oldest brother, Jim. The backward scrawl reminded me of those years when the old Bible was passed around, carried to church, and claimed as "mine" by three different boys. Mom didn't often get to carry the Bible herself while we were growing up, but we frequently found her reading it at home when we came in from paper routes or base-ball games.

The other reference on that first page was Psalm 37:4 in Mom's handwriting. I turned to the chapter and saw that Mom had underscored the verbs in the first five verses. They admonish:

"Fret not thyself because of evildoers. . . .

"Trust in the Lord, and do good. . . .

"Delight thyself also in the Lord. . . .

"Commit thy way unto the Lord; trust also in Him; and He shall bring it to pass" (KJV).

But apparently her favorite verse was "delight thyself also in the Lord; and He shall give thee the desires of thine heart."

On the next page is the inscription from Dad. "To Bonnie, in loving remembrance of October 21, 1942 — Your devoted Red. Matthew 19:6." He'd been nearly nineteen, she sixteen, when they were engaged. World War II and his thirty-two months in the Pacific delayed their marriage until December 1945.

I turned the next page. "Hello everybody." Jim's writing again, probably kindling someone's indignation. But the words were never scratched out, and they remain as a child's warm welcome for anyone who cares to open Mom's old Bible.

On the next page Jim wrote "The Way of Salvation" with a verse for each of five steps. Despite the inconsistent strokes of the preteen writer, the guidelines are still there for men of all ages who want, as Jim pointed out in step three, a "way of escape."

Scanning the pages, I noted several of Mom's markings, countless underlinings of promises and passages that look to heaven. The penciled markings had faded and the inked jottings had bled through to other pages. But the evidence remained of well-listened-to sermons and cherished hours alone in the Word.

In the back, after the concordance, the guides, and the maps, Mom listed several references to crown of joy, righteousness, life, and glory. Looking up 1 Thessalonians 2:19 showed me again that Mom loved to rejoice in the thought of Christ's return.

On the last page of Mom's Bible, she again wrote "Psalm 37:4." That last inscription is framed

by the doodling of youthful hands. One of the desires of Mom's heart was that her little boys would
grow up and do something more profitable with
those once-small hands.

Mom's first desire, she told us, was that her four
boys would make decisions to trust Christ. We
have all done that. Mom still delights herself in
the Lord, which is a continual encouragement for
me to do something constructive with the hands
that scribbled in her Bible so many years ago.

Mom's old Bible reminds me of her hands.
Hands that held, spanked, mended, and wiped
tears; hands that produced a magic knot in the
shoelaces on my three-year-old feet.

Mom's hands turned the pages of her old Bible
for me until I learned to read it myself.

DON'T KEEP THE FAITH

IN HIGH SCHOOL MY BROTHER JEFF and I had finally broken out of the spiritual doldrums and decided to live for Christ, by God's grace, even if it meant we were alone in a school of 2,500. It turned out we weren't alone, and we both enjoyed meeting new Christian friends and seeing old friends come to Christ.

But I became impressed by one older friend who seemed to have his act together. He talked a good spiritual game, even testified in church, and led singing occasionally.

Most impressive was his tract wallet. It was a big, tri-fold vinyl holder stuffed with an all-star lineup of tracts. He even had pamphlets containing entire sermons from a famous evangelist. This was no shirt-pocket wallet. It fit only in the breast pocket of a suit coat.

Every time we got together, I asked to see his tract wallet. I read those sermons and noticed on the back that others were free for the asking. I wrote to the evangelist's headquarters and asked for every sermon available.

It was a great day when those sermons arrived in the mail. I stayed up late for two or three nights, reading hundreds of sermons. They were inspiring, and I learned a lot. Then I asked my friend where I could get a wallet like his. I had never seen one before.

"You really like it?" he asked.

I said I sure did. And now I needed a convenient place for my sermon pamphlets and my own tract stash.

"You can have it," he said.

"Really? Are you serious? What will you do with your stuff?"

"You can have that too."

It was too good to be true. I told him several times that I didn't feel right about taking it, but he knew how intrigued I was with it. He said he could get more literature and another wallet. No problem.

I cherished that wallet. I took it with me to every meeting, and at home I organized it and reorganized it until I had tracts on every subject and sermons on various topics arranged like a mini-library.

It was a few months before I realized that I had never given anything away from that wallet. I hadn't shared my faith for weeks. I was so busy maintaining my little storehouse of spiritual goodies that I had become ineffective as a witness.

Younger Christians knew about my new tract wallet, and they were as impressed with it as I had been when my friend had it. They didn't know that I wasn't living up to its potential, just as I didn't realize — until later — that I had never seen my friend really use it either.

I added to it. By the time I was a freshman at Moody Bible Institute in the fall of 1967, I also carried a tiny three-ring notebook full of pithy statements like: "You can't know how good the good news is until you know how bad the bad news is."

I showed it to my new friends. One girl seemed

particularly unimpressed and kept asking kindly what its purpose was. The tracts, the sermons, the sayings were fine, she implied, but so what?

"What do you do with them?" she wanted to know.

Soon I began leaving the bulging wallet in my room. It was noticed by a friend who was impressed with it. "Don't you use it?" he asked. "Would you consider letting me have it?"

I said no to that. I didn't want it to do to him what it had done to me. I spent that evening reading through all the stuff again. The next afternoon I stuck it in a corner of my closet and accepted the invitation of some friends whose faith was not in a wallet, not in their pockets.

Their plan was not to keep the faith, but to give it away. We hit the streets.

LOW-KEY ANGEL

IF I HADN'T BOUGHT MY FIRST HOUSE from the man, he might not remember me at all. I'll be surprised if he remembers the incident I am about to repeat.

Gary Havens, a married student at Moody Bible Institute when I was a freshman during the 1967–68 school year, was editor of the student newspaper. I spent a lot of time in that quaint, cluttered office, upstairs from the Sweet Shop and next to the barbershop in a building that no longer exists.

Gary was quietly impressive. He was always dressed up, like a real adult at work. That made the rest of us want to dress appropriately too. Gary took his job seriously, and it rubbed off. We wrote and edited and thought and planned better when we worked at it, rather than when we played at it.

Though Gary could be blunt and wasn't afraid to forthrightly disagree, and though he didn't allow silliness to go on too long, we had fun. We were part of something. His standards were high. Nothing done halfway was acceptable. No one got away with treating *The Moody Student* like a typical college newspaper.

At the end of the year, that volume of the paper received several prestigious honors. More important, those of us who worked there took good work habits with us into careers and ministries.

Yet the incident I think of when Gary Havens comes to mind has nothing to do with journalism or professionalism. It has more to do with compassion and sensitivity.

During my first month as a student, I turned eighteen. Had that occurred while at home, my parents would have seen to it that I registered for the draft. As a student, I was in little danger of being called into the service, yet the law stated that I had to register in person.

A suburban kid, I was new to Chicago. Moody was a cocoon against the big city. When practical Christian work assignments took me onto the streets, buses, and subways, I was in a group, following the leader. No groups want to register for the draft. Before your birthday rolled around, your job was to get there and do your red-tape thing in the bureaucratic jungle.

I don't recall how Gary learned of my impending birthday, but one day, without making a big deal of it, he reminisced about his first confusing months in Chicago. He'd had to learn the streets, the mass transit routes, the business end of things. He must have seen a look in my eyes that betrayed the terror I would never admit.

He spoke casually. "Let me know when you have to go, and I'll run you over there."

He would run me over there? Could he have any idea how freeing those words were to my spirit? I thanked him nonchalantly, wanted to embrace him, to exult in my good fortune. The dread of this very grown-up experience was ominous enough without the trauma of simply trying to get there.

When the day came, Gary and his wife drove me to the Selective Service System office. Without condescending or belittling me, Gary walked me through the process, explaining, asking questions I would not have thought to ask, making it painless.

Before I knew it, it was over. My card—which I still have—was secured. I was legal. During the next couple of years I would still have to endure a few of the humiliating entrance examining physicals. But Gary had made the first part easy.

In the ensuing years he counseled me on when to stay or to leave an employer, sold me my first house when he and his family moved, and then lost touch. I grew up and learned the city, and now I enjoy the challenge of negotiating the maze — physical and bureaucratic.

Though it's been more than twenty-five years, I still remember how foreign it all was to me. And how grateful I was—and am—to Gary Havens.

DON'T GO DOWN THERE

IN APRIL OF 1968, I was an eighteen-year-old college student confined to an inner-city campus because of violence in the streets.

Martin Luther King, Jr., had been assassinated, and blacks in Chicago ghettos—and all over the United States—reacted with a rage born of frustration and helplessness.

After groaning about being campused, we adolescents found ways to entertain ourselves and make life difficult for our resident advisers. We enjoyed the feeling that we were all suffering together, and we actually had fun.

We rigged up a pie tin full of flour outside the elevator so a friend of ours was whitewashed when the door opened. He played it to the hilt, acting appropriately indignant when it hit him.

You see, we really had little idea what was going on outside. We had heard reports of fires and riots and looting and National Guard troops. But the sirens sounded far away. There was nothing to see on LaSalle or Wells Streets, just north of the Loop.

And so we played.

I had sentry duty on the fourth floor landing of Smith Hall as my compatriots tipped a garbage pail full of aluminum cans over the railing on the seventh floor. (I was intrigued that a couple of hundred cans fall silently, except for a slight tinkling as they brush each other in the air.) A second later they hit the basement floor like an atomic bomb.

Of course, that brought the authorities running. I hid in the prayer room. When a resident adviser burst in, I assured him, "They're not here!" He thanked me and ran off. I took the stairs to the roof.

Stepping out onto a small balcony, I could see the city from a new vantage point. Streets were closed. I was surprised to be able to hear the soft clicking of the stop lights at Chicago Avenue and

LaSalle as they changed for cars that never came.

To the south and west I heard sirens and craned my neck to see the inky sky lit up with dozens of fires. From LaSalle I heard the roar of engines and spun around in time to see a parade of military vehicles charging south, their massive, ugly bodies lined up on the double yellow line.

What was inside now seemed trivial and immature. I felt a need to be out where the real action was. This was new to everyone, and to one born after World War II, it was big stuff. I wanted to experience it, to know what it was really all about.

So I did something stupid. I took my radio press pass (I helped out in the newsroom part time) and went out. A supermarket was ablaze a few blocks away. I seemed to be the only white civilian on the streets. The looks in the eyes of the crowd running toward the fire is something I will never forget.

A blue and white squad car carrying four cops, every window duct-taped with huge Xs, slowed as it approached me. The front window came down and a pale officer spoke. "Don't go down there."

Perhaps he was cautioning me for my own safety. I waited until the squad car pulled away, then I kept walking. The cops circled the block and slid to the curb beside me. This time the officer pointed a shotgun out the window.

"Don't go down there."

That time he explained it to me better.

When I got back to the dorm, our pop can prank had been found out and my friends lectured. I took a lot of needling for having been unaccountably absent when judgment came. Yet my own sentence had already been delivered.

By having been out where I shouldn't have been, by encountering fear and danger and grief so real I could taste it, I had been awakened to the difference between flour whitewashes, aluminum can bombs, and the real things. Maybe we could all have fun again some other night.

LIFE TRACES

UNDER MY BEARD IS A SCAR that runs from the side of my mouth almost to my neck.

It's a life trace, a reminder of a horrifying middle of the night in 1968. I was eighteen, working for a suburban Chicago newspaper until the wee hours. At just before 3 A.M., I started home. My plan was to sleep until midday, then drive to Michigan for my brother's wedding. The rest of the family was already there.

I remember turning left after the last stop sign before our subdivision. I awoke in the emergency room of the local hospital, my body shuddering uncontrollably. I felt no pain, but I was cold.

Strange dreams played at my consciousness. Squad car lights, broken glass, twisted steel—got to get out, can't open the door, finally push it open against resistance. Step out onto a thrashing mass that had blocked the door, hear a whinny, step back. What is that?

A horse is writhing under my Volkswagen Beetle. I'm walking away. Someone takes my arm, calls my name. I'm sitting, then lying in cold, wet leaves at the side of the road. Now I'm walking away again.

"Is he drunk?"

"Are you kiddin'? It's the police chief's kid. They don't drink."

Something wet and cold on my face. Someone gently pulls me back. The light is in my eyes, but what are the strange dreams?

"Where am I, Sarge?"

"Emergency room, big boy. You had an accident."

"I'm havin' this dream about hitting a horse."

"You're half right. You hit two."

Horses from two nearby farms, loose in the suburbs? I had just crested a small hill as the horses shied away from an approaching squad car. I hit them head-on, knocking one out of the way, the other sliding atop the tiny, sloped car and crushing the roof into my face, then sliding back off the front and winding up underneath.

I remember nothing but the aftermath: staggering down the road in the cool night air, cops trying to get me to sit in the leaves till the ambulance arrived. I caught a glimpse of the damage to my face in the stainless steel trim of the X-ray machine an hour later. My face had been laid open. Plastic surgery and more than 100 stitches put me back together. The next day, as visitors began arriving and relatives hurried home from the wedding, I had the strangest feeling. I see it now from an adult perspective and understand better, but I am chagrined to admit that back then it was simply so puzzling.

I had the sense that the brush with death, because it had resulted in only a flesh wound — albeit a painful and disfiguring one — was almost worth the attention.

I know that sounds sick, bordering on the neurotic, but I have since learned that my feelings were not unique.

Why is it that adolescents feel so invisible and

insignificant that almost anything is worth being noticed? It isn't that I would have thought of anything so bizarre or would have consciously risked my life for the sympathy and attention it evoked. But when it happened, and all those people came, I remember thinking—absurdly—that it was very nearly a fair trade.

Up to that time I had not been aware of such a desperate teenage yearning for attention. I had loving parents, was not deprived. So this sobered me, taught me things about myself and other kids that affects how I deal with them to this day. Psychiatrists tell us that there are indeed people, and not just teens, who are accident-prone for that very reason: it's the only way they can get attention.

My goals are, first, to give kids positive attention—to notice them and encourage them; and second, to point them to the One whose attention is the only attention that really matters—the One who died for them.

LESSONS LEARNED EARLY

AT EIGHTEEN I STRUCK UP A FRIENDSHIP with the assistant manager of a fast-food place. He was a bright-eyed, open sort of a guy. Spiritual things never came up, but I looked for openings.

One day his face was lit up like noon in June. "Have I got something to tell you! It's the greatest thing I've ever heard of, and I'd be no friend if I didn't share it with you. You've got to come with me to a meeting tomorrow night."

"Well, sure, but what—"

"Just say you'll come."

I was convinced he had become a Christian, and I was depressed. Not for him, of course, but for me. This guy was more excited than I had ever been.

I told my dad—a police chief—and asked if he'd go with me. "I think I'd better," he said. "It's as likely a scam as anything. This guy naive? Interested in getting rich quick?"

"Probably, but Dad, he was as excited as a new believer."

"He is a new believer. But in what?"

We rode with my friend. And Dad was right. It was a pyramid selling scheme. Your average Joe, with a little work, a little luck, a little investment, and enough relatives could make a shade under $105,000 a year selling gyroscopes that would keep your car from fishtailing. Honest.

It sounded so good, such a sure thing, that I didn't know how anybody could pass it up. I wondered where I would come up with the money and how many my dad would buy. I could see why my friend was so excited. These people put Christians to shame.

When the pitch was over, the sales force took over. "How many would you like, sir?"

Dad was masterful. "None for me, thanks," he said.

The young salesman thought he had been prepared for every objection. "If you have any questions about the product, I can answer them."

"No questions."

"If you need financing, we can arrange that. Let me start you with one on a no-risk, fully guaranteed, money-back basis." He slid the order form under Dad's nose.

"No, thank you."

"You don't want to make $105,000 a year?"

Dad looked him in the eye and smiled. "I'm not motivated by great amounts of money."

Now there was one he hadn't heard before. "You're not? How about just the one for yourself? Do your family a favor and keep yourself safe. Keep your own car from fishtailing."

"My car doesn't fishtail. I drive slowly in bad conditions."

That valuable lesson has protected me against irrepressible sales people ever since. When they learn I'm not motivated by money, they have nowhere to go, unless their product truly is more important than the money we can both make off it.

On the way home in a steady drizzle I learned

another lesson. My friend's car was equipped with "the product."

"Watch this," he said, gunning the accelerator as he turned a corner. The car spun completely around in the street.

He was red-faced, and we were silent for the next several minutes until my friend spoke. "Chief Jenkins," he said, "if you're not motivated by money, what are you motivated by?"

What an opening.

"I consider my life worth nothing to me, if only I may finish the race and complete the task the Lord Jesus has given me—the task of testifying to the Gospel of God's grace" (Acts 20:24).

SUMMER IN DALLAS

AS I SEEM TO BE SAYING more and more in my dotage, it seems like yesterday.

Dianna and I had been married about a year and a half in 1972 and had been apart hardly longer than a few days. We both worked at Scripture Press, I in editorial, she in clerical. When the opportunity arose for me to attend Explo '72 in Dallas, we agreed I should go.

The event was a Campus Crusade for Christ extravaganza designed in part to show that there were tens of thousands of Christian young people who could be just as enthusiastic about their faith as their secular counterparts about their music.

That was the age of the mass rock concerts and festivals — magnets that seemed to attract an entire troubled generation to Woodstock and Monterey and wherever else the sound was loud, the drugs were plentiful, and love was given a chance.

Campus Crusade chose Dallas for its alternative. Kids streamed in from all over the country to study the Bible in daily workshops, to learn to explain their faith, to blitz the area with personal witnessing, and to fill the Cotton Bowl each night for worship.

At twenty-two, I was young enough to be a participant, but I went as part of the press corps. I was intrigued by the incredible variety I saw. The thousands who showed up included everything from short-hairs out of conservative Bible colleges to hair-to-your-waist devotees of Larry Norman, Christian rock, and the Jesus People.

In that one place matronly middle-agers with hefty black Bibles sat in the grass and prayed with tie-dyed teens who were only a few months out of the world of drugs.

Though it was all fascinating, the capstone of the experience was the nightly meeting in the Cotton Bowl. The stadium was filled to overflowing, including the football field. Speakers like Billy

Graham and Bill Bright, along with the best Christian music available, drew more than 80,000 each night.

The first night I went as a detached observer, eager to play my role alongside skeptics from the major news media. At press conferences, Campus Crusade publicists had tried to tell how big a potato chip would be required to feed all the attendees. Reporters from *Time* and *Newsweek* and the *New York Times* interrupted with questions about security, motives, intolerance, and profits.

I don't know how they reacted to what happened in the stadium, but I know I will never be the same. I stood in the end zone at one end of the field, scanning the crowd as the sun set. In the hour or so before the program began, spontaneous choruses sprang up from various pockets, and soon the whole place was in song.

Then came the chants. From 40,000 on one side, "Hallelujah!"

And from the other side, "Praise the Lord!"

Meaningless phrases to some, perhaps. But to a young journalist raised in the church, it was cathartic. Were there really this many believers in the world, let alone in one place?

Jesus Freaks sat lotus-style, holding hand-carved wood crosses aloft to the cheers and one-way signs of thousands. During the program, every testimony, sometimes each phrase, was greeted with cheers and applause. To hear that many people sing songs of praise was a foretaste of heaven.

The lump in my throat began early, and it wasn't long before I was unable to sing along. I just turned around and around in a slow circle, drinking it in, shaking my head, and weeping.

I was not raised in an emotional tradition, but I believe emotions are divinely given. God stirred mine that week.

I only wish Dianna could have been with me. People still ask why we named our first son Dallas. Now they know.

KINDER THAN KIND

WHEN THE FRANCIS SCHAEFFER FILM and book *How Shall We Then Live?* hit Chicago in the 1970s, I joined more than 4,000 at the Aerie Crown Theater at McCormick Place to see it.

Dr. Schaeffer was also there in person, and at the end of the film, the great Christian philosopher and thinker took questions from the audience.

At one point a young man in the balcony began a question in a halting, nearly incoherent growl. Clearly he suffered from cerebral palsy. Dr. Schaeffer closed his eyes in concentration as the question went on and on. I understood maybe one-fourth of the words.

When the man finished, Dr. Schaeffer said, "I'm sorry, I didn't understand the last three words."

The young man repeated them. "Forgive me," Dr. Schaeffer said, "the last word again, please."

After the young man repeated it, Dr. Schaeffer restated his question and answered it with the time and dignity he had accorded all the other questions. When the young man asked yet another lengthy question, some in the audience shook their heads, as if irritated that he should take so much time.

But Dr. Schaeffer repeated the process, being sure he understood every word and answering fully. It struck me that he had been kinder than the incident called for. He could have asked someone else to interpret for him. He could have asked to speak to the young man later. But everything he had expounded in his book and film was tested by this seemingly insignificant incident.

He had been kinder than kind.

A few years ago, my wife and I attended a writers conference. We were in the cafeteria, conversing with a local pastor and his wife, when a lady with cerebral palsy was wheeled to the table and her tray of food set before her.

The pastor greeted her as if her joining us was a

highlight of his day. He introduced her all around and joked with her. Somehow it came out that they had met just two days before.

The rest of us sat there trying to avoid embarrassing her, not looking as she awkwardly pushed the food around on her plate, spilled most of it on its way to her mouth, and left most of that on her face. Her new friend, the pastor, took it in stride.

He didn't look away. Without fanfare he casually put his own spoon at the edge of her plate so she could scoop her mashed potatoes without losing them. He looked at her when he talked to her, and when too much food accumulated on her face, he casually wiped it away with his own napkin.

He would have been kind to have simply included her, talked to her, and treated her as a peer. But he had nurtured her, protected her, helped her without making a show of it. He had been kinder than kind.

A couple of years ago I was at a convention waiting to chat with Roosevelt Grier, the massive former pro football player, now a minister. Just before I got to him, a woman brought her young teen son, who clearly had Downs syndrome, for a handshake and an autograph from Rosey.

The big man could have simply smiled, shaken hands, and signed. But he did more. He dropped to one knee, putting him at eye level with the boy. Rosey put his arm around him, pulled him close, and spoke to him quietly. I couldn't help myself. I edged closer.

"Are you a Christian?" Rosey asked.

"Yes, sir."

"Praise the Lord. Can I pray with you?"

The boy was overcome. All he could do was nod. As they prayed, the mother wept. When she tried to thank Rosey, he simply winked at her. Then, to the boy, he said, "You take care of your momma now, you hear?"

"Yes, sir."

Oh, that we might all be caught being kinder than kind.

FATAL CHOICE

A FEW YEARS AGO, my family lived in a Chicago suburb where a neighbor fascinated my kids. When he came home from work, his children jumped and screamed and hugged him. My own son told me, "I wish I had a dad like him."

That could have wounded me, had I not long since decided to become such a fixture around my own home that my arrival would be taken in stride. I'd rather my kids remember a dad who was always there for them than one whose arrival was noteworthy.

My wife and I knew the sad truth about the neighbor. I'll call him George. His kids were so glad to see him when he showed up, because he rarely did. He had a good job, but he often went two or three nights without returning home.

When George did arrive, he had gifts for everyone to make up for having been away. And these
weren't business trips. His wife didn't know where
he'd been either—until she got bills from bars and
massage parlors.

My wife and I discussed George until well into
the night on one occasion. I pontificated that he
needed God, needed a spiritual anchor in the uni-
verse, needed peace, joy, hope, and a reason for
living.

"How do we tell him?" Dianna asked.

I outlined a long process of earning the right to
be heard, meeting with George's family informally
and socially, really getting to know him. It all
made sense. "He needs to be desperate before
he'll come to us for help or before he thinks anything we have to say is valid," I said.

We slept well, having decided to get together
with George and his wife "sometime soon," just to
break the ice.

The next morning I was called to the phone
from a meeting. It was Dianna. "George's wife
found him in the garage with the car running. He

left a note on the kitchen table."

I could hardly speak. "Why do we always wait?"
I managed. "Why do we always wait?"

Do you know any Georges? Don't wait.

OF STICKERS AND
GATES OF SPLENDOR

ELISABETH ELLIOT'S *Through Gates of Splendor* is the story of her husband Jim and his four missionary colleagues, who were martyred at the hands of the Auca Indians in South America thirty years ago.

This is a book you read with a lump in your throat. You know the outcome, yet you plunge ahead, aware of the irony of men speaking and writing of potential danger and their relative readiness to sacrifice their lives, to meet God, to change residences. Not long into the reading, I recalled having heard recently that Paul Santhouse, then a colleague at Moody Press, had read an old Elisabeth Elliot book that had left him feeling "slain" for several days. I knew what he meant.

I pondered the value of the book, the value of the craft of writing, the power of the printed word. Moved by the lives of people who had unreservedly sold out to Christ, I was forced to compare current evangelicalism with the firebrand faith of the '50s. Men were men and missionaries were missionaries, and Christians were more interested in how well they knew God than in how well they were known.

Will it ever again be like it was in the late '40s and early '50s when myriad Christian organizations sprang up to share Christ as the answer to the needs of contemporary society? Are there but a few truly devout believers left, and do we merely tolerate them and relegate them to a super-spiritual minority?

Would we be comfortable today around a Jim Elliot, or would we be eager to toss in a religious platitude and move on to to our next amusement?

Not long after reading *Through Gates of Splendor,* I attended the Christian Booksellers Association convention, a four-day affair where publishers make book dealers aware of what's new.

There is always good and bad at these events, of

course, and sometimes it's difficult to avoid cynicism. Fifteen years ago I was introduced to Christian witnessing T-shirts (some available even for dogs!), and since then we have seen Scripture tea and even Scripture cookies.

We also saw wonderful products, books and tapes that may one day be considered classics like *Through Gates of Splendor.*

The low light of the convention for me, however, came when I passed a booth advertising Christian bumper and window stickers for your car. Some were harmless, I suppose, if you see value in anonymous, shirt-sleeve witnessing.

But other selections included "God loves blondes," "God loves Amway distributors," and even "God loves bachelors and so do I."

Ah, the power of the printed word. We have taken the medium God chose to reveal His Word to the world, and in the case of Elisabeth Elliot, we have glorified Him with it.

In the case of the stickers, I fear we have shown what truly idiotic heights we can reach.

HERE IT IS SEPTEMBER

I FIND IT AMUSING when the eyes of people born in the '60s glaze over at the mention of the assassination of John F. Kennedy, the Beatles phenomenon, Vietnam.

Do you realize that Watergate is twice as long ago to our kids than World War II was to my generation when we were in grade school in the '50s? Think of that! When my father spoke of Pearl Harbor, of Iwo Jima, of Hiroshima, of the end of the war, he was speaking of something more than twice as recent to him as my high school graduation is to me now. World War II was less than ten years old.

Twenty-five years ago I graduated from high school. Twenty years before then, the war had just ended. Skeletal survivors of the Nazi death camps had just been freed. Twenty years before that, Babe Ruth hit sixty home runs, and the stock market hadn't even crashed.

It was so recent. So recent. And it's worse heading the other way, isn't it? High school graduation seems like yesterday, and twenty-five years from now I'll be pushing seventy. I hope. My three boys will be grown, likely married, fathers. I'll be married to a grandmother.

Someone explained to me once that time accelerates as you get older because each succeeding year is a smaller fraction of your total. Makes sense. Remember how a school day seemed like years and a school year seemed like forever? Such nine-month segments now simply cause people to say, "Seems like yesterday was New Year's. Here it is September."

Here it is September. People older than I think I'm silly for feeling old, when they'd just as soon trade places. In many ways, I still feel like a kid, still getting to know my wife after more than twenty years of marriage. But I'm no kid anymore. The mirror doesn't lie.

Life is fun and funny, but melancholy when it breezes by. When I shake my head at the vapor that has already appeared for half an instant and is beginning to fade away, all I want to do is to remind myself that I could very well live again as long as I've already lived.

And I want above all else to redeem the time.

ON THE FRONT LINES

IT HAPPENED IN 1986, yet I remember the fear as if it were yesterday.

Evangelist Sammy Tippit and I had alternated driving a rented Volkswagen all day through Hungary from Austria. Our plan was to cross the border into Romania sometime before midnight.

My then eleven-year-old son, Dallas, was asleep, his mind and body ravaged by industrial strength jet lag. To him, the danger of being interrogated, detained, maybe arrested and deported to Siberia was exciting. After having slept all day, Dallas would be up all night, alert and wired for the border crossing. Having not slept all day, my nervousness — no, fear — would trick me into alertness long past my fatigue threshold. I would pay for this.

To Sammy Tippit, this was old hat. It would be his tenth border crossing into Romania. He had preached there many times. The idea of going with my old friend and taking my son had seemed dramatic, daring. Until now. The sky grew dark, then darker, then black. Dallas was up and full of questions. I didn't like Sammy's answers.

How long might we be detained? The shortest previous border crossing had been eight hours. Had anyone ever been refused entry? Yes, two laymen who tried to get in a second time were turned away; they were told they had been blacklisted because of their activities last time with Sammy. Yet Sammy was allowed through.

As we left Hungary, a border guard searched our car while we stood stamping and steam-breathing in the night air. In a friendly tone, but in a language I didn't understand, the Hungarian guard nodded to Dallas and said to Sammy, "Ah, a child."

Sammy responded in the same language, "Yes, a child."

"Oh, you speak Romanian?"

"Very little," Sammy said. It had been a *faux*

pas. An American in a car rented in the West, speaking Romanian. When the guard left, Sammy predicted he would warn the Romanian border guards a hundred yards away. My fear mounted.

The guards at the Romanian border were stereotypes. Blocky, stern, flat-faced men in uniforms, sarcastic, slow-moving, condescending, and heavily armed. One came straight to the driver's side and greeted Sammy in Romanian. It was then that Sammy knew why God had allowed a small error at the crossing out of Hungary. He was on alert. Though he knew enough Romanian to return the greeting, he looked blankly at the guard.

My stomach knotted as the man glared at Sammy, then slowly turned and walked away. We waited in the car for two more hours. Car after car ahead of us was turned away, only one of thirteen allowed to proceed. Soon it would be our turn to be searched, questioned, papers and periodicals examined, every inch of the car and our luggage combed.

I promised Dallas that I would not allow us to be separated. No separate searches, no separate interrogations, no taking my eyes off him. Excitement danced on his face; the precautions were for me, not for him.

"You're not nervous at all, are you?" I asked Sammy.

"I was earlier," he said. "The drive across Hungary, the closer we got, the more I was concerned."

"We can't get closer than this," I said. "But you're at peace. I can tell."

The windows were up against the cold. We were fogged into our own world, speaking softly. "If God wants us in Romania," Sammy whispered, "no one will be able to keep us out. If he wants us there, we'll get there. If He doesn't, we won't."

We spent ten good days there.

* * * *

We evangelicals have become a nation of fun junkies, always looking to add creature comforts to our environments. If there's anything that will cure us, it's a trip to Eastern Europe. My hope for Dallas was that he would get a view of real life. Our brief stay in Eastern Europe saw us afflicted by sensory overload that may take years to sort out.

The first church Sammy preached at was in a small town where the people seemed to have a deep joy but also a deep sense of sadness and frustration with daily life. Neither Dallas nor I had ever spoken through an interpreter before, and it was fun to communicate with brothers and sisters in Christ with whom we shared only that bond.

Gary's and Joe's brief messages were effective and meaningful, and the Lord used Sammy's powerful preaching to bring several to Christ. The local pastor was a weary laborer known for defending the rights of the citizens against the senselessness of the secret police.

I asked him if anyone but Christians were happy in this town. He struggled with the concept of happiness.

"It is not an issue here," he concluded. Happiness was not a goal, and not obtainable anyway. Joy was expressed in a smile and a greeting of "peace" (pronounced pah-chay) between believers. Poignant truth from the pulpit elicited weeping. Happiness was not an issue.

This was a land where people stood in line for a kilo of beef per month. That's 2.2 pounds. Think of it. How long would you last on the equivalent of a half pound of butter a month? A decent salary approximated $250 a month. One in ten wage earners owned a car, and all the cars are identical except for color.

Virtually everyone lived in cramped apartments, short of money, short of food, bereft of mobility (should you be fortunate enough to own a car, you could go as far as ten liters of fuel will take you each month). Power was conserved. Streets were dark. Buildings were colorless. If there was an equivalent to our Environmental Protection Agency, it was not working. Pollution blinds and suffocates.

It's dark inside and outside. Public buildings were not heated. Any Romanian who spoke with a foreigner had to report it to the secret police: names, dates, subject matter. Outsiders were followed, their inside contacts harassed. Our brief meeting with one pastor in his home was interrupted by a phone call from the secret police. He was required to come in immediately and report on his visitors.

Depressing. Oppressive. All my life I have heard

and repeated clichés about how easily we take our freedoms for granted. Being there overwhelmed me. I never felt so rich, so free, so wasteful, so extravagant.

When revival had touched cities in Romania, the picture was different. Christians were bolder, churches were packed fuller. The Second Baptist Church of Oradea began a Sunday evening service by kerosene lamp and an independent generator for microphones and platform lights.

More than 3,000 packed the sanctuary, jamming every pew, every aisle, every corridor, every room in the darkness. They stood for two hours, eyes shining, faces expectant. Fire marshals in the United States never would have allowed it.

The secret police in Romania couldn't stop it.

TV: AN EPITAPH FOR VALUES

I AM NOT MUCH OF a television watcher anymore. A few years ago, when our boys were very
small, my wife, Dianna, and I decided to neither
fix nor replace our wounded television. For a couple of years we went without.

I could recite the typical litany of improved family communications, more reading, more table
games, less hassle. All true. I'm not a militant who
encourages every family to withdraw cold turkey
from TV forever, but two couples I know well
have been without it for years, and they have
bright, productive, happy children.

We came back to television slowly. A friend
gave me one of those tiny, hand-held jobs with a
screen about an inch square. My wife still laughs

at the memory of my brother, my dad, and me cheek-to-cheek trying to watch a heavyweight title fight. When my son tried to watch twenty-two football players and a half-dozen referees on that tiny field of vision, we knew it was time to rethink our position.

We decided that our hiatus from television had been a good thing and that it had broken an addiction. Now we could own a TV and enjoy it sensibly. Our plan was to buy a nice television set, then resolve to be very selective about what we watched. I know what you're thinking, and I probably couldn't have kept that resolution either, had it not been for my wife.

It amuses her to hear people say they can't control the television or what the kids watch. Woe to a child with my surname who does not secure permission before engaging the cathode ray tube. They watch only what and when we say.

We put our new television in the basement, where it had to thaw before it could even think of warming up. Want to watch the Winter Olympics? Dress for them, then head downstairs. Even in our new house, where it's cold downstairs only because we want it that way, we choose far in advance what we want to watch. None of this let's-see-what's-on business.

So, what do we watch? Specials, sports, news, educational programs, the occasional game show (the ones based on intelligence, not luck), and the very occasional family-oriented sitcom (you know how rare those are).

Our TV is off more than it's on. Watching is a privilege earned by having homework, piano lessons, and chores done. The kids watch alone only if we are dead sure of program content. It's amazing how much discussion is necessary even after educational shows, which generally ignore the Creator and espouse evolution.

TV is worse than ever. It's difficult to brag about watching hardly anything but sports with your kids when, in so doing, you are exposing them every few minutes to sexy advertisements extolling the virtues of alcohol.

Our favorite beer commercial to hate is the one where a hunk who looks like he came off the cover of *Gentlemen's Quarterly* looks us in the eye and tells us what he believes in. Playin' hard, workin' hard, rock 'n' roll, his friends, his car, his girl, and beer. Great beer. The jingle calls it "a beer you can believe in."

There's also a car you can believe in, and a shampoo that tells you to believe in your hair.

The only way I know to fight the bad influence of TV commercials is to help the kids change the lyrics to the songs. Instead of "a beer you can believe in," they sing, "A beer you can go blind with."

Dianna has a better idea how to fight them. She knows you can't raise your kids in a vacuum, but there are days when she believes we'd all be truly better off without television. And despite the occasional great ball game or inspiring special we would miss, I fear she may be right.

FROM THE MOUTHS
OF BABES

SOMETIMES CHILDREN can be too good to be
true. I know the reverse can also be the case, but
let me stay on the positive side. One of my three
sons once told me that the wise men brought Jesus
gifts of gold, frankincense, and fur.

That was when I first became aware of how
priceless are some of the treasures that come from
the little ones. If you are raising or have raised
children, you will identify with some of the
following.

When my eldest, Dallas, was six, my wife and I
overheard him giving instructions to one of his tiny
soldiers. "You may die in this mission," he said,
"but if you're a Christian, you'll go to heaven. In
heaven you can ask Jesus for anything you want,

and if it's all right with your mom, He'll give it to you."

Chad, when eight, informed me he was going to read the Bible "all the way through."

I noticed a tiny-print *King James Version* in his hand. "That's great, Chad," I said. "How far have you gotten already?"

"Genesis 2:9."

"Wouldn't you rather have a children's Bible, something easier to understand?"

"No," he said. "You use *King James,* and I memorize out of it for Awana. I'll read this."

"It's going to take you a long time."

"Oh, yeah. I'll probably be nine by the time I finish."

A few weeks later he asked me how old Abel was when he died. "I don't think the Bible tells us that, Chad. Some people think he was a young person, maybe even a teenager."

"Hm," he said. "In my Bible, he lived only about eight verses!"

Just the other day I heard him telling his little brother, "Mike, plug in the tape recorder."

"I can't, Chaddy, I can't!"

"Mike, don't you know what it says in the Bible? 'I can do all things through Christ who strengthens me.' You can do anything!"

That convinced Mike. He plugged in the tape recorder.

Not long ago, Chad told me the story of Solomon's life, which his Sunday School class had been studying. "He could have asked God for anything, but he asked for wisdom. Then he got everything else anyway, riches and all that."

I nodded.

"But then, Dad, you know what happened at the end of his life? He blew it. He lost everything."

"It's a sad story really, isn't it, Chad?"

He looked thoughtful.

"Yeah. You'd think out of all those wives, one of 'em would've been a Christian."

ANGELA UNAWARE

YOU CAN SOMETIMES LEARN as much about love outside the church as in. Several years ago I served on the faculty of a writers conference noted not only for its training but also for its emphasis on fraternity. Writers got to know and enjoy and love one another during the week, and lifetime friendships were born or cultivated.

Angela was an outsider, a newcomer drawn by the brochure's promise of a talent night. Attendees were encouraged to bring musical instruments, puppets, object lessons, a speech, a poem, whatever they wanted.

Angela arrived plain, plump, and freshly divorced. Along with her bags was a black guitar case she insisted on carrying herself. She seemed alarmed when Talent Night did not appear in the program.

"We're flexible here," she was told. "We see how the week is going, try to determine how many are interested, and then we assign a coordinator. Are you volunteering?"

"Sure!"

Angela took her job seriously. Between workshops and major sessions, she ferreted out every actor, actress, comedian, poet, orator, singer, and ventriloquist. She drew up the program, put up posters, and made announcements at every meal.

Nearly half the conferees would perform, and I knew of no one who would have missed it. Talent Night was always a hilarious highlight.

When the big night came, Angela distributed a typed program. She had organized not only the talent but also the sound and the lighting. Those who had little talent were big on chutzpah and made us laugh till we cried. Others, accomplished at tugging heartstrings, kept us emotional.

The program went from funny to slapstick to serious, and it all led to the finale: a solo by Angela, who would accompany herself on the guitar.

That black case had made us curious, and her interest in the show made us expectant.

Angela had carefully orchestrated the show by turning it gradually more serious toward the end, when a woman did a monologue on motherhood and a man read a poem about the loss of a child. Then the lights dimmed, and Angela strode to a stool at stage center.

She knelt and removed her gleaming guitar, slipped the strap over her head, and sat on the stool, crossing her legs. She rested the instrument on her knee and tuned it. I nearly laughed when her first chord was off-key. Clearly the guitar was in tune. Her fingering was wrong. Her strum was not authoritative.

She winced and tried again. Her fingers trembled, her lips quivered. The introduction to her chorus was long but contained only three simple chords. It became evident that she knew only those three and had mastered none.

The more she tried, the more panic-stricken she appeared, and when she opened her mouth to sing, we could hardly hear her. She was short of breath, off-key, and her strumming was worse for the attention given to singing.

We agonized with her when she gave up on the guitar and tried to finish a cappella. She forgot a word and skipped it, then forgot the tune and started over.

It was then that we rallied round this sweet, tortured soul, this woman in pain who had given so much and hoped for so much. First one, then another joined her in the familiar chorus, until we were all singing, not loud but full and deep and warm.

During a pause between phrases, a man called out, "Thank you for this evening, Angela! We love you!" Three hundred stood and applauded.

Angela stood awkwardly, her hands at her sides, the guitar hanging from her neck. She tried to smile through her tears.

We had been to church.

THE MAGIC THAT DOESN'T DELIVER

I LOVE CHRISTMAS. Always have. In fact, it wasn't until I had been an adult several years that I learned that loving Christmas was not universal, even among Christians.

I was shocked to learn that many people find the Christmas and New Year season the most depressing days of their lives. My source was a Christian psychologist who had studied the problem and confirmed it in many counseling sessions.

At first I doubted him. How could this be? Even enemies seem to soften at Christmastime. Normally belligerent clerks and delivery people seem to mean it when they wish you good cheer; people do things for each other, give things to each other, seem to love each other.

But, my friend pointed out, I grew up in a close-knit family where Christmas was a time to remember, to reflect on the birth of Christ, and to epitomize the love and servant attitudes my parents and brothers and I knew we were supposed to evidence all through the year.

Think, he said, of the person who might have grown up in a tough, demanding, unloving home. Christmas, to that person, was once idealized. In spite of all his or her troubles and feelings of insecurity, Christmas carried hope.

As a little one, that person dreamed Santa would come and make everything better. Even when the disappointing truth about Santa was revealed, there was the Christ Child, and in Him was magic of some sort that makes sorrow and sadness disappear for a week or two.

Yet somehow it never lasted. No Santa, no parent, no magic could ever accomplish the permanent trick of making a person feel better about himself.

The biggest single factor leading to depression, my friend the psychologist said, wasn't the pressure, though these were contributors. It wasn't even the tension of the family get-togethers.

Rather, the most important contributing factor to Christmas-related depression remains disappointment. Too many expectations. Too much hope for magic that doesn't deliver.

As children we hope Santa or our parents will somehow know what we long for most. We shouldn't even have to tell them. We'll be good, we'll wish, we'll hope, we'll pray, and—just like in the classic Christmas movies—something miraculous will happen.

The problem, of course, is that as children, there are disappointments when the gifts don't match the Christmas dreams.

When we're adolescents, the Christmas solutions to personal crises fade or never happen at all.

And when we become adults, the hope for injured relationships to be healed, for prodigals to return, for broken hearts to be mended is dashed by the first week of January.

The one in pain may not even be conscious that he or she is really suffering a delayed disappointment from childhood of a doll that never appeared under the tree or a wind-up train that didn't compare with the electric model in the catalog.

The fact is, while God is in the business of healing such hurts, He doesn't act because of the date. He doesn't try to match the sappy coincidences the movie fantasies promise. He works in hearts, in minds, in souls in response to faith.

Do you suffer post-Christmas disappointment each year because of some unarticulated, maybe even subconscious dream that something will somehow be divinely fixed December 25?

Think about it, talk about it, dredge it up, pray about it, work toward it. The only magic in the Christmas season is in the turning of our thoughts to the greatest gift ever given or received: Jesus.

Concentrate on what He can do for others through you, and may this Christmas be your best ever.

HEDGES

I HAVE A LIST of rather prudish rules that makes me look old-fashioned and that I used to be embarrassed to speak of—except to my wife, to whom they are a gift of love.

They are intended to protect my eyes, my heart, my hands, and therefore my marriage. I direct the rules toward appearances and find that if you take care of how things look, you take care of how they are. In other words, if you are never alone with an unrelated female because it might not look appropriate, you have eliminated the possibility that anything inappropriate will take place.

I say these rules will appear prudish because my mentioning them when necessary has elicited squints, scowls, and not-so-hidden smiles of condescension. And in outlining them here, I risk implying that without following my list, I would immediately be plunged into all manner of affairs.

I don't believe that. And in enforcing my own rules I don't mean to insult the many virtuous women who might otherwise have very legitimate reasons to meet or dine with me without the slightest temptation to have designs on me.

Simply hedges, that's all these rules are. And much as people don't like to hear, read, or talk about it, the fact is that most Christian men do not have victory over lust. I have a theory about that. Scripture does not imply that we ever shall have victory over lust the way we are expected to win over worry or greed or malice. Rather, Paul instructs Timothy, and thus us, not to conquer or stand or fight or pray about or resolve, but to flee lust.

I know he specifies youthful lust, but I don't believe he is limiting it to a certain age, but rather is describing it, regardless at what age it occurs. The little boy in me, and I have room for several, will have to flee lust until I flee life.

Here then are the hedges I build around myself

to protect me, my wife, my family, my employer, my church, and, supremely, the reputation of Christ:

1. Whenever I need to meet or dine or travel with an unrelated woman, I make it a threesome. Should an unavoidable last-minute complication make this impossible, my wife hears it from me first.

2. I am careful about touching. Although I might shake hands or squeeze an arm or shoulder in greeting, I embrace only dear friends or relatives, and only in front of others.

3. If I pay a compliment, it is on clothes or hairstyles, not on the person herself. Commenting on a pretty outfit is much different, in my opinion, than telling a woman that she herself looks pretty.

4. I avoid flirtation or suggestive conversation, even in jest.

5. I remind my wife often in writing and orally that I remember my wedding vows: "Keeping you only unto me for as long as we both shall live. . . . " Dianna is not the jealous type, nor has she ever demanded such assurances from me. She does, however, appreciate my rules.

6. From the time I get home from work until the children go to bed, I do no writing or office work. This gives me lots of time with the family and for my wife and me to continue to court and date.

I share this not to boast but to admit that I'm still fleeing, and in the hope that there will be some benefit to you.

FIRST CLASS GRACE

I WOULDN'T CALL IT AN EPIPHANY, but maybe a small, not wholly adequate glimpse of grace. You stumble onto such things in unlikely places. For me it was at Washington's National Airport. This was one of those up-at-5 A.M. and home-by-10 P.M. trips. On top of that, the assignment had been unpleasant.

I was tired and must have looked it when I finally showed up at the gate so they'd know that one more pre-reserved, aisle to Chicago had checked in. All the man at the desk had to do was stamp my boarding pass, but he said something strange.

"It's Friday night, and I'm goin' home after this flight."

"Me too," I joked. But he wasn't listening.

"Let's see if we can find you a better seat, and I'll buy you a drink." He said all this while tapping at the keyboard and stamping a new seat assignment and pass.

Passengers were boarding. He wasn't inviting me to join him for a nightcap. I knew what he meant. His workweek was almost over, and I looked like someone who could use a first-class seat at no extra charge — and a free drink.

He thought I'd appreciate both, and I could tell from the look on his face that it made him feel good. I didn't tell him the free drink was wasted on me. I just thanked him.

And when I boarded, I was struck by the similarities between Christians and first-class passengers:

We were set apart.

We were there because our names were on a list.

We were treated like royalty.

We had privileges that others did not.

There were also major differences, of course, because no illustration holds up entirely:

Most had paid for the privilege. For all I knew, I

was the only one there on a free pass.

The man who showed the grace was giving me something that cost him nothing. In fact, it wasn't really his to give.

Being saved from coach class is a far cry from being saved from hell.

I sat there not wanting anyone in first class or coach to know that I didn't belong.

Maybe if there had been an easy way for many others to enjoy the same privilege, I would have shared the good news. "Yes, go see the man at the ticket counter. He'll give you a new seat assignment—free! Just ask! He wants to do it!"

Or would I have? Perhaps there are more similarities to my first-class gift and my gift of salvation than I'm comfortable to admit. Maybe I'd rather just enjoy the ride than see that others enjoy it too.

Maybe I'd rather pretend that somehow I deserved it, that I belong in God's first-class family, that I'm not here because a friendly Agent put my name on the list.

STOP ON A DIME

I HAD JUST SPENT A COUPLE OF DAYS in the home of Ron and Christine Wyrtzen. The popular Christian recording artist and her husband have an adopted daughter and son, and the very close and special relationship they all have can make you long for home.

Ron and Christine talk to their kids. They listen to them. They include them, care about them, treat them like equals. They don't pretend the kids don't need supervision, guidance, and discipline, but in the Wyrtzen home, children are people.

That environment stood in clear contrast to what happened at the Allentown (Penn.) airport on my way out of town. I sat near a mother and her four- or five-year-old daughter. Standing near us in the busy gate area was a middle-aged couple in animated conversation. As they chatted, the man pulled his hands from his pockets to gesture and a dime slipped out and bounced to the floor, rolling near his feet.

Neither the man nor his wife noticed. But the little girl and her mother did. The girl made a move for the dime, but the mother grabbed her arm. "I want that dime, Mommy," the girl whispered.

What an opportunity to teach a child ethics, fairness, politeness, courtesy!

"I know," her mother said, giggling. "Wait till they walk away."

"He doesn't see it!" the girl said.

"I know. Just wait." The girl fought her mother's grip. "Just wait, honey," she said. "As soon as he leaves, you can have it."

The man and his wife looked toward the ticket counter. The mother and daughter tensed, smiling. When the couple began to move, I picked up the dime. "Excuse me, sir. You dropped this."

The man looked incredulous. "Hey, thanks a lot."

As I sat back down, I stole a glance at the mother and child. I wasn't trying to be self-righteous or smug. A dime might seem insignificant, but I grieved for that child and the values she was learning. I could only hope her saucer-eyed look indicated that she wished she had given the dime back to the man.

There was no question about the young mother's tight-lipped scowl. She wished I'd minded my own business. I wished her daughter was my business. And despite what I tried to say with a stern return of her gaze, I'm still kicking myself for not saying anything.

Like: "Great job of parenting, lady. I hope your daughter doesn't grow up to be a certified public accountant. Or a civic leader. Or a mother like you."

Mercy. It's better I kept my mouth shut.

LOVE ON A WINTER'S NIGHT

WHEN DIANNA AND I began having children, I knew I would one day get a glimpse of God's unconditional Father love. I enjoyed reading of parents overcome by emotion, willing to do anything for their children.

Parents understand God's sorrow over broken relationships. They understand what it means to hate the sin and love the sinner. They know what it means to love someone no matter what. They learn what their parents endured, and they realize they may have been wrong in assuming they couldn't tell their parents everything.

I'd like to think my boys can tell me anything. Nothing they say or do could lessen my love for them. They're fourteen, twelve, and seven now

[1989], and I have a good relationship with each. I believe they're confident of my love for them, though I can't presume they tell me everything. I want them to feel free to talk to me about any problem, and if memory serves, our oldest is already more frank with me than I was with my parents.

I don't know what I was afraid of, but now that I'm a parent, I know I couldn't have shocked or disappointed my parents to the point where they would have disowned me. (Right, Mom?)

Parenting, with all its ups and downs and frustrations and fears, remains the most fun part of my life. Other pleasures give temporary rushes, but what can provide as deep a sense of satisfaction as knowing your child has received Christ, has learned to be kind, to think of others first, to work before he plays?

What could be more gratifying than to hear a child say, unsolicited and unprompted, "Love you, Dad"?

Our youngest, Michael, is currently the most cuddly. He's a lanky first-grader who still has a baby face. He never lets me get out the door without a "Hug/kiss! Hug/kiss!" He's also still excited when I pull into the driveway in the afternoon, running to jump into my arms.

It was Michael who prompted my latest rush of emotional love. I had put him to bed an hour before. Dianna was at a meeting, and Dallas and Chad were at piano lessons in town, ten minutes away. Dianna and I discussed the possibility that Michael would be asleep when it came time for me to drive in and pick up the other two.

Should I just let him sleep, assuming he wouldn't stir during my twenty-minute absence? What could happen? We came to no conclusion before Dianna left, so when the time came for the run into town, the decision was mine.

The downside of taking him with me was that I would interrupt his deep, sound sleep, which any child needs. The four of us would just barely fit in my small car for the ride back. What could happen if I left him? A prowler? A fire? A water problem?

You can imagine how brief was the mental debate. I crept into Michael's room, gathered his quilt about him, and lugged him out into the wintry night. Dead to the world, he wrapped his arms around my neck and breathed heavily in my ear.

I could have held him like that forever, but I had to set him down to shut the back door. I scooped him up and deposited him in the car, where he immediately stretched out in the backseat.

Halfway into town, I heard him stir. He raised his head.

"What's my blanket doin' here?"

"You're sleeping, Michael. We're going to pick up the boys."

When we got there, he sat up to make room. The older two chattered about their lessons, and Michael laid his head in Chad's lap. They didn't notice that I wasn't upholding my end of the conversation. I was overwhelmed with love for my boys and moved by the thought that my Heavenly Father loves me even more than that (Matt. 7:11).

A DAD BY ANY OTHER NAME

SHE CALLS ME HONEY and I call her babe, but when she or the boys talk about me, they all call me Dad. Dianna wouldn't say, "Go ask Honey to come upstairs," or, "Go ask my husband." She doesn't even call me "your dad," as many mothers refer to their husbands.

I'm just Dad. It's my favorite name. Oh, it's embarrassing when Dianna forgets that my lunch bag doesn't have to be differentiated from thirty others—like the kids' lunches do—and writes DAD on it in big, block letters. But I still like the name.

I'm Dad to my fourteen-year-old. Someday I'll be Dad to all of them, and I'll miss the Daddy part. When I once shaved off my beard, Michael said, "Now you look like the real Daddy!"

I'm still young enough to be uncomfortable being called Mister. When I hear "Mr. Jenkins," I look for my own dad. Though being called Dad reminds me that I can remember Dad when he was my age, I have to let it sink in that I play the same role with my boys that he played with his.

He was, and is, everything to us. It didn't impact my brothers and me that he was raised without a father, until we were grown and had children of our own. We can't imagine having grown up without a father. And I'm sure my brothers wonder, as I do, at what a father he was and is, considering he had no model.

Our family has a strange custom. Though we are all relatively outgoing and social-minded, when we get together—even after having not seen each other for months—we seem to take each other in stride.

The lack of enthusiasm in our greetings doesn't mean anything. It surprises people who expect us to embrace or exult, but that's just something we've never done. Yet feelings run deep. I sense as much affection in our casually picking up conversations — and relationships — where they left off as I would in a joyous reception.

Part of that, of course, comes from Dad. He's a humorous man and an articulate poet, but not overly expressive. "Still waters run deep" and "strong, silent type" are the clichés. A man's man, a Marine, a police chief, still he is always polite, soft-spoken, considerate, a gentleman.

He doesn't consider it old-fashioned to open a door for a woman or to rise when she enters the room. He's been told he's "honest to a fault" — quite a commentary if you think about it.

Best of all, he's been a one-woman man all his life. If it's true that the best thing a father can do for his children is to love their mother, my brothers and I had the best thing done for us from the days we were born. Dad is an unabashed romantic and proves his love every day.

He was a model in his willingness to scrub floors, change diapers, cook, or do whatever else needed doing when all four boys were home and Mom needed help. He was never too much man for that. He didn't just tell us what to do.

It's said we get our first and most lasting image

of God from our fathers. That makes me grateful. Grateful that my dad is not an alcoholic. Grateful that he is faithful. Grateful that he is industrious. Grateful that he loved his sons unconditionally and proved it more than once.

I'm grateful Dad's priorities are right and un-compromising. Grateful that he cares more about people than things, more about family than money, more about loyalty and integrity than image.

He's not perfect like the Heavenly Father. But to have half his character is my loftiest dream. To be thought of one day the way my brothers and I think of our dad. . . .

The only thing he didn't teach me was how to comfortably tell him out loud that I love him. But I do, Dad.

PARENTING 101

BASEBALL SEASON becomes football season, and that turns into basketball and soccer seasons. Before you know it, spring baseball will be here again. If you're a parent, the whole year is one big carpool season.

We complain about it, but in truth Dianna and I love it. Once we've figured out who goes where and when and who will watch which kid, we settle into our lawn chairs and enjoy.

Usually I meet the family at the game on my way home from work. Dianna brings healthy munchies to tide us over. It's all great fun and I'll never forget it, even if the kids do. Which I doubt they will.

Seven years separate our eldest and youngest of

three boys, and Dallas, fourteen, has already pledged that, like his dad, he will always make it to as many of Michael's games as possible. "He's had to sit through all of mine," Dal explains.

It's heartwarming to see brothers support and encourage one another. I suppose it's helped that Dallas has had his sport (basketball), Chad his (baseball), and Michael his (soccer, so far). But they really are proud of one another. Attending one of our kids' games is one of the funnest things we do together.

Win or lose, we're all in it together. It's a priority. It's also a lesson for all of us. In nearly every game we see examples of good sportsmanship and bad sportsmanship. We see coaches (fortunately usually only opposing coaches) who care more about winning than about having fun or developing character or teaching fundamentals.

We see good players who are lazy and bad players who hustle. We see the occasional good player who hustles, which makes him great. We see (and hear) fans who know how to encourage and cheer and be good sports, and we see (and hear) the opposite.

Our favorite bad example of a parent/coach was in charge of a visiting team. Apparently he had been a great baseball player in his day. He was embarrassed by the performance of his players, and he said so, loud and often and from all over the field.

He carried on a play-by-play harangue of every missed opportunity, every taken strike, every bad throw or missed ball. Admittedly, there were many. His team was inept. But they were young and eager. That eagerness died as the game wore on.

They fell further and further behind, and their spirits were broken by the endless badgering for all to hear. The players made blunder after blunder, their eyes cast down, their shoulders stooped. And the coach continued, "That's no way to throw! I'm embarrassed! If you can't do any better than that, you might as well sit down! I've never seen anything like this in my life!"

But then, a miracle of miracles. With the bases loaded, several runs already in, and two outs, one of our hitters drove a sky-high pop-up toward second base. The shortstop on the ill-fated team circled beneath it, fear on his face.

At the last instant he stabbed at the ball and it stuck in his glove. His teammates cheered. Even our fans applauded. He looked expectantly at his coach. Surely this would earn some morsel of praise.

"If you'd missed that one, you'd have run forty laps tomorrow!" the coach said.

What a sad picture. If it's true that our views of God come from our parents and others in authority over us, imagine what those players think of Him.

In life we're all players on a bad team. We try. We fail. We mess up. We sin. But our eyes don't have to be cast down, our shoulders don't have to be stooped. Our Coach takes us as we are and makes us into something better. And what do we hear?

"Well done, good and faithful servant."

We parents and coaches can take a lesson.

THE LESSON IN
THE SHELLS

I WAS ON MY WAY BACK to the United States
after a trip to Irian Jaya. I'd gone there to observe
relief efforts after the 1976 earthquake. The jum-
bo jet had landed on a runway that dominated a
tiny South Sea island—one of those inexplicable
stops that are neither for picking up nor dropping
off passengers, or even taking on fuel.

Airline personnel herded us under a wind-and
sun-faded wood canopy where we sat on benches
with our cameras and our fatigue. On three sides
of us lay hundreds of yards of shell-strewn sand
and the beauty of the endless sea. Behind us
wound a few narrow streets of squalor.

Almost immediately, we were besieged by the
island's bronzed children. They had long, jet-black

hair, dark eyes, and gleaming teeth. With their hands full of shells, they hard-sold everyone.

"Dollar!" they said, and they laughed when people looked shocked. "Nickel!" they said, giggling. Some people bought shells they could have picked up themselves a few feet away.

"Don't do it," an older man said wearily. "These kids are supporting their parents' drug habits."

I had been so used to declining the beggars who had lined the streets in Irian Jaya that it was easy to turn away these little paupers. One boy started at a dollar and went to fifty cents, then a quarter, a dime, a nickel, and even a penny before he gave up. I didn't need or want any shells, and though I enjoyed him and smiled at him, I shook my head. He moved on to success with someone else.

At the edge of the tiny sales force stood a little girl with a face so radiant I will never forget it. She couldn't have been more than five years old.

When the rest moved on, she continued to stare at me, then she approached, her tiny hand crammed with three shells, each about the size of a golf ball. She smiled and held out her merchandise for me to see. I smiled and shook my head.

That's when she said the word in her own tongue that I could not understand. I assumed she was saying "cheap," or "dollar," or "deal." I shook my head again and she reached closer. She pleaded with me now, repeating the word over and over.

How these kids have been trained to pull at your heartstrings, I thought. I would not be moved. I shook my head again and saw her tears form. Very well done, I thought. Almost worth a sale. But no. I was too sophisticated for that.

She moved away from me with shoulders slumped and tears streaming. She squatted nearby and cried, not looking at me. She had me; she had won. I pulled two dollars from my pocket and went to her.

What was this? She wept even more, and now it was she who was shaking her head. And she repeated the word.

Confused, I went back and sat down. I leaned over and interrupted a missionary's kid involved in another conversation to ask her what the word meant.

"It means 'free,' " she said, turning back to her conversation.

I was stunned. No wonder I had so saddened the little girl. I approached. She looked at me warily. I pulled my hands from my pockets and showed her my empty palms. Then I repeated the words as a question, and she beamed as she handed me the shells.

DEAR GRANDPA:

IT WAS GOOD TO SEE YOU RECENTLY,
even though when my brother Jim and I walked in,
you weren't sure at first which of your relatives we
were. I could tell you recognized us as two of your
twenty-four grandchildren or fifty-plus great-
grandchildren, and we didn't mind your asking,
"Which one's your mother?"

Our mother is your fourth child and second
daughter, Bonnie. I can imagine that at age nine-
ty-two it's hard enough to remember your own
seven surviving offspring, let alone theirs.

I can't imagine that I will ever forget those wonderful times we spent at your huge, old home in
Wisconsin when I was a child, but should I be
blessed with as many years as you, perhaps I will.

Neither can I imagine ever forgetting your investment of time and money to self-publish a collection of the cute things your grands and greats have said over the years.

I thought of your special project the other day when Michael, our youngest, who just turned seven, told me that he knew Jesus' name. "It's Amen, right?" he said.

He has a little trouble with Satan's former name too. "When he was an angel," Michael said, "his name was Nicholas or Christopher or somethin' like that."

A delight in children has been one of your life's hallmarks. You were never too busy, never too important, never so self-absorbed that you couldn't hold one on your knee and giggle at his antics.

You loved to see the little ones learn to walk, and now you're justifiably proud that you are one of the few in the nursing home who can get to the dining room on his own. The voice is weak, the gait is deliberate, and the memory is not what it was. But that sly smile, that glint in the eye, tells me it's still you.

I've always appreciated your sweet, gentle spirit and your deep love and interest in your friends and family. You might be surprised to know how much I brag about your creative genius.

It was thrilling to see your paint-by-numbers projects in various stages of production and to know that you're still active. I'd love to play Scrabble with you or hear you play one of the many musical instruments you invented and so enjoyed performing. We'll long cherish the videotape of one of your last extended shows, wowing them in the church basement on your musical gadgets.

I was surprised to see how strong and clear your handwriting is, especially after you wrote that you are gradually getting weaker.

It saddened me that you wrote, "Really, I would like to go to sleep and forget to wake up," but I can certainly understand.

I'm sure it feels as if your most important and productive days are over. Perhaps you're bored now with what seems to be simply biding time. Rest assured that if you do forget to wake up some morning, you'll be sorely missed by more people than you can imagine.

Meanwhile, those of us who love you don't begrudge you the wish to see again your son, your wife, and—for the first time—your Savior face to face.

We love you so much and will miss you so much, that we selfishly want you to stay with us forever. But we ask only that you have as much faith and confidence now in the sovereignty of God and in His timing as you had when you trusted Him for your salvation and for the guiding of your stellar life. That's our answer to right-to-die advocates.

We usually are hesitant to raise the subject of your preceding us to heaven, but of course, we all wonder every time we see you whether it will be the last time.

I get to Kalamazoo infrequently now, and who knows, I may have already seen you for the last time. I hope not, but should that be the case, I'll see you at one of the twelve gates of pearl.

FOR "BABY" MICHAEL

HEY THERE, LITTLE LEAGUER
In the dead of night
Jump quickly from the covers
'Cause you've had a fright.

The lightning and the thunder
Send a flash, crack, boom!
Chase a tiny third baseman
To the master bedroom.

On the baseball diamond
You show lots of nerve
But a midnight storm
Tosses you a curve.

In truth you make your daddy
Feel brave and strong
Happy to protect you
The whole night long.

You're the little fellow
Who came along last
Keeps Mom and Dad young
And ties us to our past.

This month you'll turn eight
Though you were born yesterday.
We'll prob'ly pray for more storms
Before you're grown and away.

    This verse came to me in the night, with the little guy beside me in bed. I had always thought my dad was the only poet of the clan. Maybe this proves that he is; I was intrigued by the cadence until I realized that it's probably a rap. No more, I promise.

    We try not to baby our youngest. I know what it's like to be the last of three. I was grateful when my little brother came along when I was 10. Suddenly I was one of two middle children rather than the forever baby.

Michael's at that age when his little body seems a perfect reflection of what God had in mind for us. He's lean and wiry, strong and fast, not an ounce of fat. His face is open and trusting, his smile sweet and quick. He's still young enough to allow us to touch him, and his face is soft as a baby's.

Michael still likes me to sing him the lullaby I made up for him when he was an infant. You can apply any simple tune:

Nighty-night, Little Mike,
Everything is all right;
Mom and Dad and Dallas and Chad
Love little Michael.

Nighty-night, sleep tight,
Everything is all right;
God and Jesus and Mom and Dad
Love Baby Michael.

THE STIRRER
OF THE SOUL

WHAT IS IT ABOUT MUSIC that so moves the soul?

The other night our church got together with two sister churches for an evening of music. I was not expecting the wonderful experience that resulted. I enjoy congregational singing and have even sung in small groups and choirs. However, I simply looked forward to an enjoyable evening.

Soloists, duets, trios, quartets, ensembles, and choirs from each church performed in turn, with a little congregational singing sprinkled throughout. Those I talked to afterward seemed to agree that it was one of the most special nights they had spent in a long time.

I am not a musician. If the truth be known, I

respect and admire musicians to the point of envy. My mother is a piano student and teacher, a choir director, a soloist. My brothers and I endured the obligatory years of beginner piano books that prove you were raised in an evangelical home. (I got as far as "The Happy Wind Sock.")

I have always loved to sing, but I have rarely performed with fewer than two others, because alone I would be unable to draw enough breath to be heard. I don't know how soloists do it.

And though I can follow the little black dots and occasionally even recognize which one someone is talking about when he refers to it by letter, I can't say I "read" music.

But there's something about music that lifts and inspires.

As I tried to analyze what it was that people from all three churches so appreciated about the musical evening, I kept coming back to the familiarity of the old hymns we sang. There were plenty of old hymns, along with a lot of contemporary music for the younger people.

Years ago, while in the throes of a childhood illness, I was serenaded by my now late maternal grandmother, playing the piano in her staccato style and singing to me in her lilting soprano, "We'll talk it over, in the by and by. We'll talk it over, my Lord and I. I'll ask the reasons, He'll tell me why, when we talk it over in the by and by."

I also remember my mother, able to get time alone at the piano only after her three elementary-aged boys were in bed, playing such hauntingly beautiful melodies that I would sometimes pad out in tears and ask her to play something different.

During the early years of married life, before Dianna and I had children and when I would often write till midnight, I sometimes turned on a late talk show to unwind for a half-hour or so. On two of those programs, years apart, I heard songwriters tell of their lonely vigils, picking out notes, sometimes writing a song every day or so till that 100th or 200th combination of lyric and notes would make sense and become a standard.

Though my discipline was entirely different from theirs, for some reason those songwriters inspired me with their dedication to craft. One was Jimmy Webb, who wrote the wonderful music to "My Beautiful Balloon." The other was a country artist who wrote dozens of hits.

He told of being up in the middle of the night experimenting with notes and chords on the piano when a song came to him. He played and sang it softly, weeping at its beauty, then woke his wife and asked her to come and listen. They both wept as he sang and played.

That story made me want to stay at my work until something like that happened to me. Because that writer's success wasn't magic or luck. It came from a lifetime of doing the little things right, of dedicating himself to his art and taking no shortcuts.

Because we are to live our lives as unto the Lord, all work is Christian work, and we should present our very best to God.

Someday we'll see what a beautiful thing He can make of it.

AGES AND STAGES

IT'S FUN TO HAVE BOYS. Michael, the youngest, reminds me of the purity and innocence and wonder Dallas and Chad exhibited at his age. The teenagers foretell what the little guy will become.

Michael still thinks it's a thrill to see his dad walk past his schoolroom. He'll wave and might even shout before I can shush him. He's not afraid to hug or be hugged in public.

Recently I decided to take him with me on an overnight business trip. I found it a fascinating weekend, ten hours in the car and several other hours watching him interact with adults.

"Sorta fun and sorta boring," was his typically honest assessment. But there was no boredom for me. That much uninterrupted time in the proximity of such an uninhibited mind is a delight.

Michael would catch me gazing at him and smiling. "Oh, Dad," he would say, sighing. "You're sittin' there lovin' me again."

Mom had packed his stuff—clothes, toys, books, tapes, and tape player in his own bag. I tried to convince him that even if his ears didn't hurt, he could hurt his ears by playing his Odyssey tapes too loud through the headphones. "If I can hear it, it's too loud," I said.

"How much longer?

"I'm hungry.

"I'm thirsty.

"How come sugar is worse than protein? What's protein anyway?"

Later, I asked, "You wanna talk, Mike?" ·

"In a little while. Right now I'm doing some repairments on my Legos."

"Maybe Uncle Jim could help you. He's handy, and his kids had Legos."

"Maybe. But didn't he live in the olden days?"

Jim is three years older than I, so I guess he did.

"Dad, what am I supposed to say, again, when Mom asks if I had a good time?"

"Not 'Sorta boring, sorta fun.' "

"No. I had a grrrreat time with Dad!" He thought that was pretty funny. He knew Mom would know better.

Michael is at the age where he likes to be the one who prays for meals, prays for a safe trip, prays for people. He is full of questions about heaven, a new heaven and a new earth, what, when, how, why. How I wish his questions, questions, questions didn't reveal how little I know.

On the trip home I had to choose between the interstate, which is farther but often smoother, and coming through Chicago. I chose Chicago, and I chose wrong.

Just after I had breathed a silent prayer of thanks for a smooth, quick trip, the traffic stopped. For half an hour we crawled through narrowing lanes. Then the lanes would widen, the pace quicken, and we would think it was clear the rest of the way—only to come around a bend and see the taillights of a thousand cars.

I tried to draw a spiritual application, forgetting that the hours and the traffic had extended him past teachability. "This is how life is," I said.

"Smooth and easy, then a jam, frustration, wondering if things will ever be back to normal."

I droned on about expecting the unexpected, not being fooled by temporarily smooth sailing. Michael was playing with the seat adjustment, trying to stretch out. While we stopped, I let him unbuckle and scamper into the backseat where he could lie down.

"Learning anything?" I asked.

"Yeah. Don't work in Chicago. Don't drive in Chicago. Take the train. Or bring more tapes."

The day will come when those lanky limbs of his will fill that car. He won't be hugging me in public or squealing an excited hello. I'll be taking him, or riding along as he drives, to college or farther. That trip will be just as precious, but more melancholy.

I'll miss him. Especially the nine-year-old version who will always remain in my heart.

WAGING THE WEIGHT WAR

FRIENDS AND FAMILY SAY that the 130 pounds I lost have taken several years from my appearance. My hope, of course, is that the shed pounds will add several years to my life.

Losing that much weight was interesting and exciting, especially because it happened fast (the first 100 pounds in 17 weeks). The process also involved risk, fear, and psychological stress.

I reduced the risk by going through a physician-monitored hospital program. Still, an all-liquid, high-protein, low-carbohydrate diet pushes the body into ketosis where it literally feeds on itself for energy. Auto-cannibalism is dangerous.

My fear comes from the odds against long-term success. Some experts say that only 1 in 1,000 who lose more than 100 pounds will keep it off for more than a year. The most common question is, "How will you keep it off?" There's only one way, of course, but for some reason, hardly anyone succeeds.

Someone asked if I am confident I can do it. The only thing I'm confident of is that I'm determined to succeed, with God's help. Though I have enough of an ego to believe I could be 1 in 1,000, I am also realistic and humble enough not to be overconfident.

(Consider Oprah Winfrey and others like her who certainly could not lack for motivation or track records of achievement, yet cannot gain a long-term victory against this common problem.)

As for psychological stress, I've been amazed. No one is fat on purpose—I never planned on being the largest person in most of the circles I run in. So I was unaware of the presence and power that accompanies size until I lost it. Despite the clear health benefits, at first I irrationally felt less significant.

Behaviorists say that people who lose weight quickly need time to catch up with their images in the mirror. I see the thinner face and body, but I do not "own" them yet. I finally understand the anorexic who looks like a death camp inmate yet sees a fat person in the mirror.

I enjoy the attention that comes with my new look and the achievement of a difficult goal, but I also look forward to that day when people take the new me for granted.

The hard part comes now. As difficult as the losing was — especially because I did not cheat an iota — keeping it off is clearly the bigger challenge. It's a war, with food as the most hypocritical enemy, smiling as it stabs me in the back.

Every obese person is aware of the physical reasons for his weight. I never cease to marvel at the well-intentioned who think they're breaking news to a fat person by suggesting some form of discipline, lifestyle change, reduction of intake, or increase of activity. Duh.

We know. Trust me, we know better than most.

What does the struggler need? Acceptance is the key — unconditional love for us just the way we are: fat, medium, or thin. Admittedly, that's a tall order, but it is a godly model, isn't it? My wife has modeled that acceptance all our married life, and it has been the greatest of all motivations.

People with weight problems know their loved ones want them alive and healthy. We are always on the edge, however, of wondering whether looks or even words of encouragement have hidden, conditional meanings. That is unfair and irrational of us and may hint at the psychological reasons for obesity. The subject is worth a book, which I may try if I succeed over the long haul.

Meanwhile, I make no promises or guarantees except that I will wage the war. The best help anyone can offer is prayer and confidence. I will be grateful for either from you.

DEAR SON:

IT'S FUN TO SEE A RELATIONSHIP budding. You have discovered someone who cares about you, and vice versa, and so now you have a huge responsibility not only to each other, but also to each other's loved ones. I've always admired your standards, and now they will be put to the test.

Her family and your family love her and you, but as you progress there are two unknown, unnamed, and probably unrevealed people you should be thinking about just as conscientiously. I'm referring to your respective future spouses.

I know your relationship is embryonic, but as you enjoy getting to know each other better, you may very well start thinking about your future together.

You will give no greater gift to her and to her eventual husband than that she enter her marriage a woman of pure character and control—not just physically a virgin, but also pure of thought and word and action.

What may in time seem to you as sincere expressions of love and affection should be seen in the light of the future. How you talk to each other, what you dwell on, what you watch and read and say and even joke about should be things that honor God and become wonderful memories of a special relationship.

Most of all, your relationship should leave each of you with no regrets: nothing you would be ashamed to take with you into marriage.

The odds are very much against the prospect of your marrying someone you dated as a teenager. That's why my emphasis is on your future spouses, given the probability that they will not be the two of you.

You know that I was involved in a lengthy relationship and was even engaged to be married before we broke up and eventually married other people. How grateful I am for the provision of

God, the purity of that woman, and the way we complemented and counteracted (as appropriate) each other's strengths and weaknesses.

I haven't seen my former fiancée for more than two decades, yet I would be able to look her and her husband in the eye and be proud that we did nothing we had to regret or hide from our spouses.

That required strategy, foresight, planning, and care. We heard enough, cared enough, and knew enough to stay out of situations that would test our will power past reasonable limits.

At some point you will soon start imagining, wondering, contemplating, toying with the idea that you might indeed become each other's future spouse. It happens. All the more reason to follow the above advice. Think of your future spouses all the time, even if they are you. Don't fall into thinking, "Hey, it's going to be just the two of us forever anyway," as if that justifies anything.

As I say, the odds are against that happening, but if that is God's will, you'll have given each other the greatest wedding present anyone can give: pure minds and bodies and hearts and consciences, having proven your dedication to God on the tempting battlefield of real life.

Your greatest advantage is that you come from families who care deeply about such matters and aren't afraid to talk about them. All four parents will be honored and thrilled if you stand with that ever shrinking minority that goes against the grain and does the right thing because it's the right thing.

No excuses, no alibis, no rationalization, no pointing the finger and saying, "Everybody does it," no easy ways out.

There are reasons for God's clear prohibitions in the area of sexual purity, and as with every biblical restriction, the payoffs for obedience are that much more rewarding than any temporary pleasure.

May you maintain your standards. We love you with all our hearts and want only the best for you. And may you do the same for the one you care about, because she is no less loved by her family.

Love, Dad

TEMPUS *CERTAINLY* *DOES* FUGIT

ON THE OCCASIONAL TIMEPIECE, usually a grandfather clock, you might see the Latin phrase *tempus fugit,* which I'm told means "time flies."

When I was a child, time flew only when the long hours of school and chores (my major task was trying to get out of them) ran into that hated word, bedtime!

Even summer vacations seemed long. For some reason, those ten weeks between academic years seemed like years in themselves. I have as many memories from summers as I do from all the months in school. That will come as no surprise to my teachers.

But now the days whiz by, and all those dire predictions by my elders are truer than I ever dreamed. They told me—the same way I tell young parents—that I should enjoy my children fully because they're here one day and gone the next.

Dianna and I look forward to an empty nest someday—sorry, boys—but how frightening is the truth that our children will be so soon gone.

In this wonderful day when fathers are present at the births of their children, each emergence of a squalling life was burned into my mind and even deeper onto my soul.

My boys' births seem as if they were only months ago and weeks apart. I remember Dallas' (sixteen) every bit as clearly as Michael's (nine). But when did Chad (fourteen) become a teenager? Wasn't it last summer that he was a cherubic blond with hair we should have cut before it curled below his ears?

No, that was more than a decade ago.

Physically, I aged young. My father is finally grayer than I, though my two older brothers are not. I have to concentrate to see the lines in Dad's face. I always think of him as a young father.

And my mental image of my mother has probably lagged at least twenty years.

It's easy to see both ends of the family the way they once were: robust young parents and cuddly toddlers. But the mirror is hard to fool. I'm older than my image of my father. My nieces and nephews are becoming parents, my brothers grandparents.

My oldest son is now taller than I; number two will soon shoot past me. I'm tempted to put some sort of growth-stunting device on the head of the little guy, but I know there will be no slowing him either.

What I want for them and for me is that we not just note the passing of time. I want us all to be able to look back periodically and do more than simply shake our heads at the *fugit*ing of *tempus*. I want us to see growth and development and redemption of the days.

The older I get, the simpler my philosophies become. I'm not smart enough for them to be theologically deep. Yet even some of the more academically brilliant minds I know have seemed lately to focus more on the basics.

As the calendar pages waft by, I want to be less

satisfied with such growth as becoming a daily flosser, a seat belt wearer, a food label reader, and an obnoxious nutritionist (my family is long-suffering with this newcomer to fitness.)

I want to work before I play, but be sure to play every day. Even more important, I want the profound truths to which I subscribe to be obvious in my speech and my life.

God loves you.

God cares about you.

Jesus died for your sins.

Jesus is alive.

Jesus is coming again.

That's as profound as it gets, but in light of those truths I know I must keep short accounts, develop the inner life, mend relationships, and make known the faith.

Tempus fugit.

ADDICTED TO ANTICIPATION

CHRISTIANS ARE, by the nature of their faith, inveterate anticipators. I have always been addicted to the future.

As a child I looked forward to my next birthday, to the next summer vacation, to the next ball game, the next special event, the next, the next, the next.

There was a period when I felt guilty about that. Someone would speak on the need to be content in Christ, to relax and find peace in Him, to not always need a picnic or a party or a meeting to anticipate. What was wrong with me, I wondered, that I always needed something in the future to keep me from a vague, unsettled feeling?

Over the years I tried to change, but without

success. I resonated more with ministers like War-ren Wiersbe and George Sweeting, who often emphasized that the Christian life was a series of new beginnings. Being like Christ was the goal. Thus the journey required—and allowed—a fresh start every day.

Maybe there is some sort of psychological health in having down time, nothing pressing, nothing tangible to look forward to. But I've never found peace in that and have decided to quit trying.

Those who spend every minute planning the next rush, the next high, the next activity that will keep their minds occupied, should slow down and become introspective occasionally. Clearly something is wrong with a person who feels a desperate need to fill his days so he doesn't have to face himself.

But anticipation, looking forward to good things, is part of our heritage, our legacy. Because God's mercies are new every morning, forgiveness awaits us. Our humanity, our frailty, need not weigh on us so heavily. We anticipate tomorrow with its fresh supply of mercy.

Sure, some people ignore the admonition of Paul and attempt to "go on sinning so that grace may increase" (Rom. 6:1). Yet such a storehouse of mercy should never be seen as license, but rather freedom—freedom to serve with pure hearts despite old natures.

Because I know that God knows me and understands my frame and remembers that I am dust (Ps. 103:14), I can look forward to tomorrow. I can anticipate good things. I can even anticipate hard, challenging, difficult times that will result in growth.

I no longer feel guilty for always needing to look forward. Believers are to live in the present with our eyes on tomorrow. Striving to serve Christ in spite of ourselves is the stuff of our lives. We can begin afresh and anew every day.

By the end of this decade I will turn fifty—which seems younger all the time. My wife and I, should the Lord tarry and spare us, will be empty nesters. As much as we love our sons, we look forward to that new adventure.

We anticipate seeing them finish high school, choose college and/or career, fall in love, marry, become parents. We look forward to the continual growth of our own relationship, now beginning its third decade of marriage.

There are things we want to see, things we want to do. There are people God will put in our paths for various reasons: some for us to help and some to help us. The future, with its events and its personalities, even its uncertainties, lies ahead like an uncharted sea.

Pain and disappointment are certain, as are health problems and even death. Yet these things merely reinforce our addiction to the future. Jesus told His disciples, and thus us, that He has gone to prepare a place for us. "I will come back and take you to be with Me that you also may be where I am" (John 14:3).

Dianna and I dream of building our own place one day. It will be fun and exciting to have more to do with a home than merely "finding" it. But may the enjoyment of that endeavor serve only as a microcosm for what awaits us on that great day when we see Jesus.

We're addicted to the future, because when that endless tomorrow arrives, all else will pale.

MEMORIAL MEMORIES

"IT'S NOT WHERE YOU START, it's where you finish—and you're gonna finish on top!"

We don't hear that old song in church, but perhaps we should. True, it espouses a you-can-do-it theme, but what can be truer of the Christian's state than that we finish vastly different than we begin?

I may be too young to be thinking about finishing well, but we never know when we might finish. I take great comfort in the fact that the work of Christ is complete and that I don't have to scramble to be, or even appear to be, perfect in the end.

No, it isn't for the sake of hanging onto my salvation that I long to keep maturing spiritually. We should all want to reflect positively on the reputation of Christ, not to earn salvation but rather to live out our gratitude for that ultimate gift.

I'm reflective and preoccupied with such things just now because I recently returned from a memorial service in honor of an older saint I had known for years. Actually the service was in honor of his God, which is the way Peter Gunther would have put it.

Pete was not a perfect man, and no one who eulogized him pretended that he was. He was, however, a forgiven man who lived in relentless pursuit of serving God through the printed page. During the middle of this century he worked with Ken Taylor at Moody Press and Moody Literature Ministries. The two of them traveled the world, putting Christian books in the hands of people who might otherwise never have benefited from such material.

Taylor, of course, went on to paraphrase *The Living Bible* and found Tyndale House Publishers. Peter Gunther retired from Moody in the early 1980s and moved on to Colorado Springs, where he headed up international relations for the Christian Booksellers Association. It was in Colorado where he died of cancer and was remembered by many of his colleagues.

I was struck by two things as I heard the eulogies. The first was that the service might not have been quite so solemn and dignified had Pete been there in person. Although he was devout and serious and even emotional about his faith, he also displayed a refreshing sense of humor.

The eulogies made brief references to Pete's love of jokes and to his occasional stammer. But I remember once when he opened in prayer at an editorial meeting, asking that God grant us "clear thinking and—" There he stopped, unable to think of the next word. He hesitated, started, stopped, and started again, finally dissolving into laughter and admitting, "I think I just got the answer to the clear thinking request!"

I feel privileged to have known a man so single-minded in his commitment to serving Christ.

He started humbly in a huge family of modest means. Today he lives in a mansion, just over the hilltop.

It's not where you start; it's where you finish.

THE ARM IN THE NIGHT

WHEN I WAS A CHILD one of the highlights of my week was playing tag in the parking lot after church on Sunday nights. We kids would burst from the tiny sanctuary of the Oakwood Bible Church in Kalamazoo, Michigan, and race between the cars.

I was one of the youngest and smallest (we're talking a long time ago), and so my only advantage was speed and trying to be the first one out. I was under strict orders not to run in church and not to move until the final "Amen."

One Sunday evening found our family propitiously sitting near the back, with me closest to the door. When the service was over I strode as quickly as was legal to the foyer, bounded down the

steps, and shot through the door into pitch darkness. No one else was even close. I took a hard left
and sprinted with all my might toward the parking
lot.

Suddenly I was stopped in my tracks by what
felt like a huge arm at my waist. I felt like a car-
toon character who'd hit a railing. My hands and
feet flew out ahead of me, but I had stopped. I
immediately assumed one of the men of the
church had snared me and would warn me to slow
down.

I spun around sheepishly to take my lecture, but
from whom? Would it be big Walt Burke, a neighbor and once my Sunday School teacher? Or old
Mr. Kemple, a pillar of the church? No one was
there. I squinted until my eyes became accus-
tomed to the light and realized I was standing at
the edge of a ten-foot hole.

How could I have forgotten? The entire parking
lot had been excavated that week. We were building a new sanctuary, and the men in the church
had been helping. I had seen my own father in
that hole, helping pile the concrete blocks that
would become the new building.

There were no construction horses or warning lights or streams of tape to keep anyone out. Who but a child would forget the parking lot was now a cavern with piles of bricks at the bottom?

I turned rubbery-legged and moved back toward the church door. By now the other kids were pouring out. They were running the other direction. They had all remembered. How could I have missed that the street was lined with all the cars that used to fill the lot?

More important, what had stopped me at the edge and saved me from certain injury and maybe death? I was too shaken to play and just stood there deep in thought. It was several minutes before the first adult emerged from the church.

For many years I wondered. I put the strange experience in the category of something in a dream that makes you twitch or jerk and wake yourself. You don't know what it was, but it affected you.

It was only when I heard similar stories later that I began to realize that I had been the beneficiary of divine intervention. Coming from a tradition less than enthusiastic about experientially based faith, I was slow to make the connection.

But as I searched the Scriptures—which I firmly believe are the test of experience, rather than vice versa—I became comfortable with the idea that guardian angels do protect the saints. Most often we are likely unaware of their intervention, but at times, the evidence is stark.

I am wary and suspicious of those who say they converse with angels and focus their attention on them. Yet I am thrilled and inspired by stories of modern-day protection.

Cannibals ask missionaries, "Where did you get that army dressed in white that encircled your camp every night when we wanted to kill you?"

A mugger tells the police, "I ran when the girl began praying because of all those men who suddenly surrounded her."

I have stopped trying to explain away the arm in the night that kept me from plunging ten feet onto piles of bricks.

"For He shall give His angels charge over thee, to keep thee in all thy ways. They shall bear thee up in their hands, lest thou dash thy foot against a stone" (Ps. 91:11-12).